MW01201655

POLAR REGIONS

By Lorraine Hopping Egan

Please Return To:
Barbara Wierzbicki

SCHOLASTIC
PROFESSIONAL BOOKS

NEW YORK • TORONTO • LONDON • AUCKLAND • SYDNEY
MEXICO CITY • NEW DELHI • HONG KONG

DEDICATION

*The author would like to thank Louise Spigarelli,
whose dedication to teaching social studies
is longitudinally unparalleled.*

Cover design by Pamela Simmons
Text and interior design by Sarah Morrow
Interior illustration by Patricia J. Wynne
Photo Research by Sarah Longacre
Poster photos: Polar Projections: © Jim McMahon/Scholastic; Ice Floe © Super Stock; Inuit Man © David Hiser/Tony Stone; Arctic Fox © Wayne R. Bilenduke/Tony Stone; Caribou © Super Stock; Antarctica © Franz Lazi/Photo Reseachers; Amundsen-Scott Base © David Millar/Science Photo Library; Emperor Penguins and Adelie Penguins © Super Stock; Antarctic Fur Seal © Art Wolfe/Tony Stone; Arctic Tern © Laurie Campbell/Tony Stone

ISBN 0-590-76248-6

CONTENTS

The activities in this book correspond to the National Geography Standards and themes of location, place, movement, region, and human/environment interaction.

LAUNCHING A POLAR REGIONS UNIT

Bundle up! You and your students are about to explore the coldest places on earth—the polar regions. This book contains everything you need for a successful cross-curricular unit: accessible background about major polar concepts, exciting activities, reproducible pages, book links, quick facts, and even some polar jokes to share with children!

Here are a few ideas for making the most of your polar journey:

Enhance Your Learning Center

In this unit you'll find several items and activities that could anchor a Polar Regions Learning Center. Included are the polar poster (insert), the polar animals card game (page 39), and polar puzzlers (page 7), which challenge students to discover new things about the poles. Display the poster at the center, along with artwork and projects that students complete during the unit.

Take a Polar Journey with Books

How can students experience the polar regions without sub-zero temperatures, blinding snowstorms, and expensive equipment? The books listed through this unit (look for "Book Links") can guide students through the frozen tundra without fear of frostbite!

Create a "There and Here" Scrapbook

How are the polar regions like your region? Most likely, they're extremely and incredibly different. As students learn about the world's extremes and about their own region, collect pictures and facts into a "There and Here" scrapbook. Each section of the book could compare and contrast a different feature such as climate, wildlife, terrain, and inhabitants.

Have fun on your polar adventure!

EARTH'S EXTREMES

MAPPING AND LOCATING POLAR REGIONS

On a planet of six billion people, very few humans ever travel to the ends of the Earth—the North and South poles. Scientists, explorers, and wealthy tourists are among the lucky few.

What's at the North Pole?

At the North Pole, you'll find a permanent layer of ice on top of the Arctic Ocean. The arctic region is mostly ocean, bordered by three huge, populated continents (Asia, Europe, and North America.) Not a soul occupies the extreme Arctic, though the lower arctic latitudes are relatively bustling with modern towns.

What's at the South Pole?

Antarctica is a huge continent separated from all other landmasses. A mere handful of scientists overwinters at bases in Antarctica. The South Pole has a science station, but no native plants or animals. Humans are the only large land animals able to adapt to the climate.

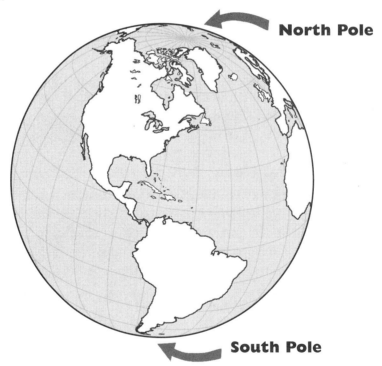

North Pole

South Pole

Exploring Polar Frontiers

At the dawn of the 21st century, Earth's polar regions are still remote frontiers. From our comfortable latitudes near Earth's bulging center, we can form a mental map of the North and South poles. The principles of geography will take us there.

ACTIVITIES
MAKING A MENTAL MAP
(geography)

As you begin your geography unit, use a globe to emphasize that the poles are literally the "ends" of the Earth—top and bottom.

With this exercise, students can make a mental map of the North Pole and find out what it's like to stand on top of the world. To begin, have students stand up and face due north. (Use a compass to find due north, or try the activity on page 8.)

Ask students to imagine that they are walking north and eventually come to a point where they can walk north no farther. They will be standing on the Geographic North Pole (90°N latitude). Ask students to look around and consider the view from the top of the world. Guide their journey with these questions:

> **JOKE**
>
> How do Russian explorers get to the North Pole?
>
> *By Bering Strait.*

1. What direction are you facing? Which way does your compass point? (South—and only south. Every way you look leads eventually to the South Pole. The compass doesn't work because you're too close to magnetic north.)

2. What's beneath your feet? (Ice that is twice as thick as you are tall, perhaps more.)

3. What's beneath the ice? (Frigid ocean with little life in it. Not enough light and nutrients reach the Arctic Ocean to sustain elaborate food chains.)

4. Do you see any signs of life—humans, animals, or plants? (None at the North Pole.)

5. If you drill straight down through the Earth, where do you come out? (The South Pole.)

6. Is it dark or daylight? (The region experiences 24-hour dark from September 22 to March 20, and 24-hour daylight the rest of the time. Each pole sees only one sunrise and one sunset per year.)

7. What does the landscape look like? (Miles and miles of open ice, cracked in places.)

EXTENSION ACTIVITY

As you progress through the unit, repeat the "Making a Mental Map" activity and see if students can add more details as they learn more. You may also wish to try this activity using the South Pole.

BOOK LINK Before starting the activity, read the first chapter of nature writer Barry Lopez's *Arctic Dreams* (Scribners, 1986). The author's vivid descriptions of arctic life will provide detailed imagery for your mental-mapping experience.

FINDING DUE NORTH ON A SUNNY DAY

(geography)

Materials tall stick

How can you get to the North Pole? By walking due north, of course. To find due north using the sun, students can do this simple activity.

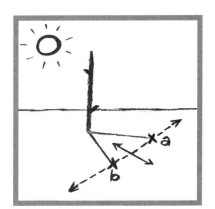

1. Go outside and pound a tall stick into flat ground.

2. Mark the tip of the stick's shadow.

3. Wait 15 minutes and mark the tip of the shadow again.

4. Draw a line to connect the two points. Stand on the center of the line, facing away from the stick. You are facing due north!

Why does this work? The sun appears to travel from east to west across the sky, so the two shadow marks form an east-west line. The first mark (a) is west, made by the sun when it is east of its later position. The second mark (b) is east, made by the sun after it has traveled a bit to the west. The east-west line is always perpendicular to the north-south line.

POLAR PUZZLERS

(science, geography)

Materials Polar Puzzler Cards (pages 13-16)

Like the mental map, the Polar Puzzlers on pages 13 to 16 can serve as motivators and evaluation tools. (Cards 1-10 are a bit easier than cards 11-20.) Post the questions on a bulletin board, perhaps covering a large, polar-related picture or collage. Discuss—but don't reveal the answers right away; let students wonder and hypothesize.

Throughout the unit, remove cards as students discover the answers. As the polar picture underneath is slowly revealed, challenge students to guess what it is. After all the questions have been answered, have students create more questions based on what they have learned. Then use all the questions for review (see "Culminating Activities," pages 75-76).

I AM STANDING ON TOP OF THE WORLD

(poetry, writing)

Materials I Am Standing on Top of the World reproducible (page 17) • blank index cards • construction paper • markers

Make copies of the poem on page 17 (one for each student, plus a few extra). Divide one copy of the poem by lines, cut the lines apart, and distribute one line per student. (Duplicate the lines if you have a large class.) Randomly ask students to read their line (in any order). By reading the poem out of order, students will focus more closely on the meaning of the words. What is this poem about? What words hint at the subject? Can students assemble the lines back into couplets? the couplets back into a poem?

Collect the lines and hand out whole copies of the poem. Have students read the poem and write the final couplet. For a greater challenge, ask students to write a short poem of their own about being on the bottom of the world. Then have students illustrate their poems and mount them on sheets of construction paper.

EXTENSION ACTIVITIES

✳ Ask students what they would take if they were packing for a trip to the North Pole. List items on the board. Then discuss which ones are most vital.

JOKE

How do farmers get to the North Pole?

By hog-led dogsled.

✳ Every explorer needs a flag to plant when reaching a destination. What might a flag for the North Pole look like? Ask students to design a North Pole flag that could represent the Arctic region.

✳ While students pretend to be "on top of the world," have them write and decorate a post card to a friend.

✳ Have students take a class opinion poll about vacationing in the Arctic or Antarctic. Which place would they rather visit? Graph the results. Repeat the poll at the end of the unit.

BOOK LINKS *Imagine Living Here: This Place Is Cold*, by Vicki Cobb (Walker, 1989). Informative introduction to all things arctic for primary readers. Charming illustrations.

The Book of Where: or How to Be Naturally Geographic by Neill Bell (Little, Brown, 1982). Humorous, hands-on introduction to geography.

LATITUDE ATTITUDE

(using a globe, research, art)

Materials Latitude Attitude reproducible (page 18) • six globes • reference books on countries, such as an almanac and encyclopedia • six shoe boxes • art supplies for creating dioramas (such as tempera paint, tissue, cardboard, cellophane, modeling clay, glue, tape, and glitter)

Latitude lines run east and west on the globe and measure the distance north or south from the earth's equator. By studying lines of latitude on a globe, students can learn more about the geography closest to the polar regions and compare it to the geography farthest from the polar regions (the equator).

1. Point out to students your location on a globe. Write the latitude on the board. Trace the latitude line around the globe and name each country you cross. What kinds of places are at this latitude? Explain that you'll be finding out the "latitude attitude" of latitude lines on the globe by seeing what kinds of places can be found at each line.

2. Divide the class into six groups and distribute the reproducible and globes. Groups will locate and record the names of countries at major northern latitudes, starting with the equator.

3. Instruct students to look for patterns in their data. Ask: How are latitude lines closer to the North Pole different from lines that are farther south? (Arctic latitudes are much shorter than temperate or tropical ones. They have fewer countries and cities.) Discuss reasons why it might be easier to live at more temperate latitudes.

4. Assign each group one of the latitudes on the worksheet. Each group should choose a different country or region to investigate at its assigned latitude.

5. Instruct each group to create a diorama showing the people, the climate, and the terrain of the country or region they've chosen to research. Provide a variety of art supplies and encourage students to show as much detail as they can with their dioramas.

6. When the dioramas are finished, write the latitude numbers on each side of the shoe boxes. Stack the dioramas from the equator (bottom) up to the North Pole (top).

EXTENSION ACTIVITY

Repeat the process above using southern latitude lines. Ask students to make predictions about what they will find on these lines. Will lines near the South Pole resemble the North Pole in any way? Have students record and compare their results.

JOKE

What did the father iceberg say to his new baby iceberg?

Just go with the floe!

THE ARCTIC VS. ANTARCTICA
(geography, reading a chart, research)

Materials The Arctic vs. Antarctica reproducible (page 19) • Polar Regions poster • encyclopedias and nonfiction books about the poles

Both the southern and northern extremes are frigid, icy, and as far away from civilization as one can go and still be on solid ground. Yet the Arctic and Antarctic are two very different places. These differences can be found in the climate, terrain, ecology, and many other aspects of each polar region.

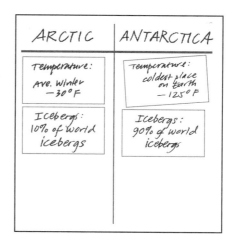

In the reproducible, students are asked to fill in a chart that shows the differences between the two regions. Students may find the answers to some of these questions by referring to the poster. They may also use encyclopedias and other nonfiction sources to complete the task. You may wish to divide the class into groups and have students in each group research the answers together, or assign each group one space on the chart to fill in.

EXTENSION ACTIVITIES

✳ Using index cards or sheets of paper, create an Arctic/Antarctic chart on a bulletin board using the column headings on the reproducible and students answers. As you progress with the unit, continue to add facts to the chart. Some other areas for comparison include temperature (the average arctic winter temperature is 30 degrees below zero; Antarctica is the coldest place on Earth and can drop to 125 degrees below zero in the winter); icebergs (The Arctic has about 10 percent of the world's icebergs; Antarctica has 90 percent); and plant life (many plants grow on the arctic tundra, including grasses and mosses; very few plants can grow in Antarctica).

✳ Here's a great opportunity to turn a popular preschool game—what doesn't belong?—into an elementary-level challenge. Gather images of the Arctic and Antarctic from this book and other resources. Put together sets of four images in which one is out of place. For example, show a penguin, a mountain, the South Pole station, and a polar bear. Ask students to pick out the one that doesn't belong (the polar bear).

TEACHER TIP

For a great take-home activity, send students home with the reproducible and one or two books about polar regions. Give students and parents a week to fill in the chart together.

THE SEVENTH CONTINENT

(map reading, social studies)

Materials The Seventh Continent reproducible (page 20) • globe

For tens of thousands of years, humans have lived on six continents. The seventh continent—Antarctica—was uninhabited and unclaimed until the 19th century. The map on page 20 shows which parts of Antarctica have been claimed by different countries. You may wish to guide the class in a discussion as you explore the questions on the map.

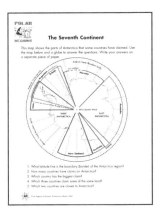

1. Distribute copies of the reproducible to the class. Discuss the purpose of the map. What does it mean for a country to have a claim on Antarctica? What reasons might the countries have for claiming the land?

2. For question 1, explain that a boundary or border is a line that separates one area from another. It can be an imaginary line, or a tangible thing, such as a river or mountain. See if students can locate the boundary of the region—the Antarctic Circle (66.6°S). The political boundry set by the Antarctic Treaty is 60°S.

3. Discuss the next three questions. Eight countries have claims (question 2). Locate these countries on a world map. Are there any patterns? (The countries are either northern European or close to Antarctica.) Australia has the biggest claim—by far (question 3); Britain, Norway, and New Zealand follow (4).

4. Discuss question 5. Chile, Argentina, and Britain claim the same land. Which country, if any, has the best claim to the land? How would students solve this dispute? Use a globe to show that Argentina and Chile are closest to Antarctica. Does this fact give them any more right to stake a claim? What are other reasons to stake a claim? (got there first; settled it first; powerful and rich country; will use the land for peaceful purposes only)

EXTENSION ACTIVITIES

❋ Compare the peopling of Antarctica to the westward movement in the United States. How do regions and boundaries change? Why do people move to harsh lands? (for a better life; to find land, gold and other valuables; out of scientific curiosity)

❋ Ask students to imagine being president of one of the countries with a claim on Antarctica. Instruct students to write a letter, explaining why their claim is valid.

BOOK LINK

Explore Antarctica, by Louise Crossley (Cambridge University Press, 1994). This extremely useful fact book includes numerous maps, charts, graphs, and photos on the geography and science of Antarctica. Produced by the Australian Antarctic Organization.

Polar Puzzler Cards

Following the dashed line, cut out each Polar Puzzler card. Then fold in half along the dotted line and glue together.

POLAR PUZZLER #1

Which continent has the southern most desert in the world?

ANSWER #1

Antarctica. A desert is any region—hot or cold—that gets very little snow or rain. Parts of Antarctica haven't had rain or snow for two million years!

POLAR PUZZLER #2

The arctic tern spends almost its entire life in daylight. How does it manage this trick?

ANSWER #2

It migrates from pole to pole, spending summer in each hemisphere. The sun shines 24 hours a day during the polar summer.

POLAR PUZZLER #3

What's the biggest land animal in Antarctica?

ANSWER #3

A tiny fly called a midge. Antarctica's bigger animals live part or all of the time in the sea.

POLAR PUZZLER #4

The word arctic comes from the Greek word meaning "bear." The Greeks never saw an arctic bear. But each night, they saw another type of bear. What was its name?

ANSWER #4

The constellation Ursa Major (commonly called the Big Dipper), which means "big bear."

POLAR PUZZLER #5

Some modern people have eaten mammoth meat. Mammoths died out long ago. So where did people get the meat?

ANSWER #5

In the Ice Age, dead mammoths froze in ice. The ice preserved them. Humans find these frozen bodies, defrost them, and sometimes eat the meat!

Polar Puzzler Cards

 **POLAR PUZZLER #6**

Why don't polar bears prey on penguins?

 **ANSWER #6**

Polar bears live only in the Arctic, where there are no penguins.

POLAR PUZZLER #7

Why is Antarctica at a much, much higher elevation than the Arctic?

 **ANSWER #7**

Antarctica is a land mass with plateaus and mountains. The Arctic is an ice-covered ocean. It's at sea level.

 **POLAR PUZZLER #8**

Antarctica is mostly rock and ice. Why doesn't it have much soil?

ANSWER #8

Soil is composed partly of organic matter (dead and living plants and animals). Antarctica is too dry, too cold, and too salty for many life-forms to exist.

 **POLAR PUZZLER #9**

Little snow or rain falls in the Arctic. Yet much of the land is filled with rivers and lakes. Why?

 **ANSWER #9**

Because the ground is frozen, rain stays on the surface until it runs off or dries up. (In warmer climates, rain seeps down into the ground.)

 **POLAR PUZZLER #10**

If it's noon where you are, what time is it at the North Pole?

ANSWER #10

Any time or all times! All 24 time zones meet at the poles.

Polar Puzzler Cards

 **POLAR PUZZLER #11**

In polar regions, blizzards can form even when it's not snowing. How?

  **ANSWER #11**

Blizzard-force winds (35 miles per hour or faster) pick up snow that has already fallen.

 **POLAR PUZZLER #12**

Icebergs can be clear, blue, and sometimes green. What sea creature turns icebergs green?

ANSWER #12

Algae. It sticks to the ice underwater. Then the iceberg flips upside down.

 **POLAR PUZZLER #13**

Why do scientists sometimes find the prehistoric remains of warm-weather plants in Antarctica?

ANSWER #13

Antarctica once had a much warmer climate. The continent wasn't always at the South Pole.

 **POLAR PUZZLER #14**

What color are polar bears?

ANSWER #14

They look white, but their skin is black and their fur is transparent (see-through).

POLAR PUZZLER #15

The location of the North and South Pole changes from year to year. What causes this to happen?

ANSWER #15

The Earth wobbles a bit as it spins. When it does, the location of each pole moves in the opposite direction. (Hint: Spin a top and observe the tip. Does it stay in the same place?)

Polar Puzzler Cards

 **POLAR PUZZLER #16**

Why is Antarctica colder than the Arctic?

 **ANSWER #16**

The Arctic is an ocean. Antarctica is a landmass. Water doesn't get as cold as land. Many coastal northern lands are warmer, including Alaska's Aleutian Islands.

POLAR PUZZLER #17

What is the best month to start a trek to the North Pole—and why?

 **ANSWER #17**

March: The polar ice pack hasn't melted yet, making a solid surface to travel on all the way north and back. Also, days at this time of year are longer and warmer than in winter.

 **POLAR PUZZLER #18**

The South Pole gets only an inch or two of snow each year. How can the ice there be a mile thick?

 **ANSWER #18**

The snow never melts. It just piles up year after year. The layers compress (squeeze together) to form ice.

 **POLAR PUZZLER #19**

How does a penguin's black-and-white coloring help keep it safe from enemies? What is this coloring called?

 **ANSWER #19**

The penguin's coloring is called countershading. It helps camouflage the penguin when it swims in the sea.

 **POLAR PUZZLER #20**

Many Arctic animals such as lemmings grow up faster than their southern cousins. Why?

 **ANSWER #20**

The summer growing season is much shorter. Animals must grow up and have families before the harsh winter arrives.

Name: _____

Read the poem. Then finish the poem by writing a couplet—two lines that rhyme.

I Am Standing on Top of the World

I am standing on top of the world.
I plant my flag and watch it unfurl.
Due south and south and south I face.
Never east, west, never north do I pace.

I am standing on top of the Earth.
But I'm not standing on solid earth.
The white polar ice, one story thick,
Floats over an ocean named Arctic.

I am standing on top of the globe,
Wrapped in a cocoon from head to toe.
Each short, puffy breath hangs in mid-air.
Then freezes instantly on my hair.

I am standing on top of the planet.
In two short steps I can circle it.
For six months in summer it's lights on.
For six months in winter it's lights out.

I am standing on top of a sphere.
Nothing can ever be north of here.

Team Members: _____

Latitude Attitude

Find each latitude line on a globe. Trace the latitude all the way around the Earth. What oceans, continents, and countries does your finger cross? Make a list for each latitude.

90° North

75° North

60° North

45° North

30° North

15° North

0° (equator)

POLAR REGIONS

Name: _____

The Arctic vs. Antarctica

The Arctic and Antarctica are different in many ways. This chart shows information about both places. Can you fill in the missing spaces in the chart? We've filled in some of them for you.

THE ARCTIC	ANTARCTICA
WHERE IS IT? Farthest place North.	**WHERE IS IT?** Farthest place south.
WHAT IS IT? Frozen ocean surrounded by frozen plains called tundra.	**WHAT IS IT?**
ALTITUDE? Sea level.	**ALTITUDE?** High altitude (9,550 feet)
PEOPLE?	**PEOPLE?** Only a few scientists and tourists stay here.
LAND ANIMALS? Many, including moose, foxes, and caribou.	**LAND ANIMALS?**
WATER ANIMALS?	**WATER ANIMALS?** Penguins, seals, and whales.

The Seventh Continent

This map shows the parts of Antarctica that some countries have claimed. Use the map below and a globe to answer the questions. Write your answers on a separate piece of paper.

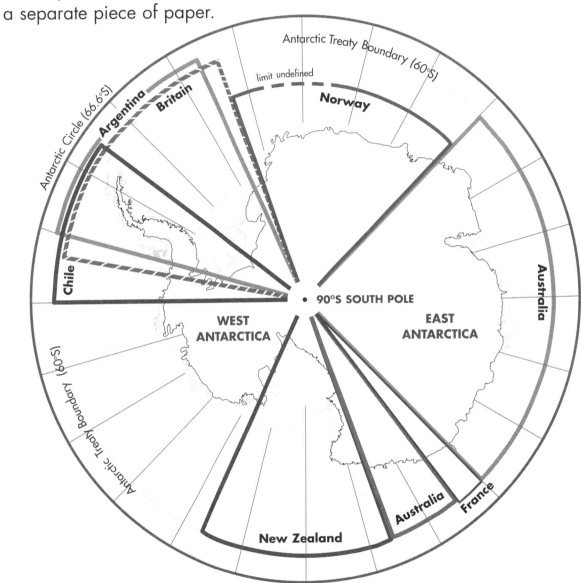

1. What latitude line is the boundary (border) of the Antarctica region?
2. How many countries have claims on Antarctica?
3. Which country has the biggest claim?
4. Which three countries claim some of the same land?
5. Which two countries are closest to Antarctica?

ICY-COLD DESERTS

PHYSICAL TERRAIN AND CLIMATE

Both the Arctic and Antarctica are ice-covered polar regions that receive little precipitation per year. In Antarctica's Dry Valleys, no moisture has fallen for two million years! The entire continent is as dry as the Sahara Desert.

The polar regions are also total opposites (see "The Arctic vs. Antarctica" on page 11). Antarctica is a continent surrounded by ocean; the Arctic is an ocean surrounded by continents. This crucial difference affects the ice, the climate, the ecology, and more.

Icy Habitats

About 98 percent of Antarctica lies under as much as three miles of ice. This icy shroud makes up about 90 percent of all the ice on Earth and about 70 percent of all the fresh water. The ice has piled up on the continent snowflake by snowflake for millions of years, never melting, always being compressed by gravity's pull. Scientists can look far into Antarctica's past by taking an ice-core sample straight down through the layers and then analyzing what each layer—or each slice of time—contains.

In contrast, the polar ice pack (sea ice) of the Arctic measures a mere 10 to 15 feet thick. In winter, it spans the Arctic Ocean, bridging arctic lands. In summer, it shrinks in half, exposing the Arctic Ocean once again. Ice covering arctic land melts into a slush during spring and summer. Underneath this ice is permafrost—permanently frozen soil that has maintained a below-freezing temperature continuously for at least two years. The melted ice can't drain easily through the permafrost, and so the icy desert turns into a watery desert of lakes and rivers.

Land vs. Water

Land gets—and stays—much colder than water. The giant landmass of Antarctica (slightly bigger than Australia) is like a freezer that can never defrost. The ice-on-rock South Pole has typical temperatures well below zero— -58°F, or -50°C, for example. In comparison, the ice-on-water North Pole is balmy, at about -4°F, or -18°C.

Bodies of water moderate the temperatures of coastal areas worldwide, bringing cool water to tropical climates and warm currents to polar regions. The Aleutians of coastal Alaska enjoy a much milder climate than inland Alaskans.

Another area in which to contrast water and land is altitude. The Arctic is mostly at sea level and the air at sea level is thicker (has more densely packed molecules) and moister. In contrast, Antarctica has the highest average elevation of all the continents— thanks to its blanket of ice. It is a very high plateau. Visitors to the South Pole must adjust to the altitude as they would on a mountain.

FACT

Permafrost in northern Siberia is about a mile deep.

Parts of Antarctica are so dry, so devoid of life, and so cold that they look and feel like the planet Mars with an atmosphere. Scientists have exploited that fact to test Mars vehicles, to study how minute life-forms in rock can withstand the climate, and to train astronauts.

ACTIVITIES

NO RAIN, NO DRAIN

(science)

Materials No Rain, No Drain reproducibles (pages 29 and 30) • soil, pebbles, sand, and clay (about two or three cups of each) • small, identical flower pots (two per group) • measuring cup • access to a freezer • basins or pans • photos of a rain forest and tundra trees (optional)

In the arctic tundra, permafrost (permanently frozen ground) blocks rainwater from draining. As a result, the tundra doesn't drain ("no rain, no drain"): It gets very little rain, but has large lakes, rivers, and peat bogs (shallow areas of soil and water that are inhospitable to life).

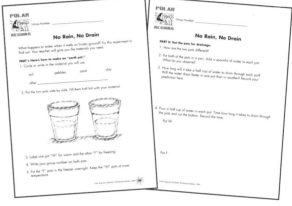

In this activity, students can find out how frozen earth affects water drainage. Divide the class into groups of three, number the groups and distribute the soil, clay, sand, and pebbles. Give each group a different material. Students can follow the directions on the reproducible on page 29 to make two identical "earth pots."

After the class has performed Part 1 of the activity, instruct them to observe, record their results, and compare their findings with other groups. Direct the discussion by asking such questions as: How fast does the water "disappear"? Where does it go? Do the pots drain equally fast? What might make a pot drain faster or slower? Which of these pots most closely represents permafrost? How did this experiment show us how Arctic lakes and rivers are formed?

JOKE

Why do mountains take millions of years to wear down?

They're in peak condition!

BOOK LINK

Disappearing Lake: Nature's Magic in Denali National Park, by Debbie S. Miller (Walker, 1997). Text and photos allow readers to observe the Alaskan water cycle.

MILE-HIGH ICE

(reading a diagram, science)

Materials   Mile-High Ice reproducible (page 31)

Antarctica's ice sheet varies in thickness, from no ice to nearly three miles of ice. The cross section on the reproducible shows the dramatic ups and downs present in the ice sheet. Make a copy of the reproducible for each student and distribute. Discuss the following answers as a class.

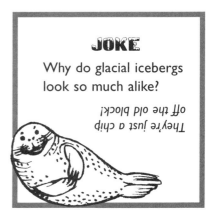

1. The top of the eastern antarctic ice sheet is highest.

2. The Transantarctic Mountains are the highest land features. They cross Antarctica, but only their peaks are visible.

3. Most of the land is below sea level (the "O" point on the left-hand scale). The extremely heavy ice actually presses the land down.

4-5. The ice sheets have smooth, dome-shaped tops. The wind has sculpted them that way. The land is very jagged and uneven; much of it is not exposed to the forces of erosion.

EXTENSION ACTIVITY

Read the lines below, which are from Samuel Taylor Coleridge's 19th-century poem "The Rime of the Ancient Mariner." It is about Antarctica. Coleridge based his poem on reports by the explorer Captain Cook, who never laid eyes on the continent. Nonetheless, his imagery, as translated by Coleridge, vividly describes the dark, icy journey toward Antarctica.

> The ice was here, the ice was there,
>
> The ice was all around:
>
> It cracked and growled, and roared and howled,
>
> Like noises in a swound*

swoon or hysterical outburst

After reading the lines, ask students to imagine what it might be like to be in such an icy place. Would they like to explore Antarctica? Why or why not?

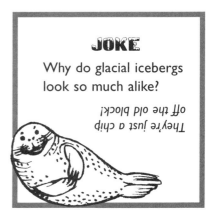

JOKE

Why do glacial icebergs look so much alike?

They're just a chip off the old block!

FACT

Ice covers a tenth of the Earth's land. At the peak of an ice age, it would cover three-tenths.

GLACIERS GO WITH THE FLOW *(science)*

Materials   Glaciers Go with the Flow reproducible (page 32) • newspaper • copy paper or butcher paper (no larger than 11-inches by 17-inches) • tape • corn syrup or molasses • waterproof markers

1. Copy and distribute the reproducible on page 32. Use it to start a discussion about what glaciers are and how they travel.

2. Spread newspaper out on a table. Crumple a piece of paper into a ball and let it relax. Without smoothing the paper, carefully pull out the corners and tape them down on the newspaper. Have students examine this "instant landform."

3. Ask students: Where are "mountains" or high points? What about plains, valleys, and plateaus? Is there a "continental divide" (peaks that send ice, or water, down to seas in opposite directions). Color these features with a marker as you identify them, choosing a different color for each type of landform.

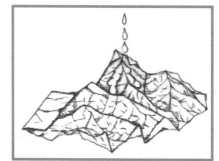

4. Together choose a steep "mountain" with several crevasses, preferably not too far from the "sea" (the edge of the paper). Ask students: If ice formed on top and started to flow, what path would the glacier take? Where might it stop? Invite volunteers to trace the path with a finger.

5. Place two drops of corn syrup on the "mountain." Explain that each drop is like the uneven buildup of snow and ice. Add drops as needed to keep the glacier flowing. Watch the syrup flow and have students compare it to the diagram on the reproducible. Discuss the ways in which it moves like a real glacier. (It flows in fits and starts; the bottom forms a "tongue"; once syrup starts down a path, more syrup follows easily—little or none veers off course; the path is skinny in steep areas and it pools in flatter areas; the liquid flows faster in the middle and more slowly at the edges.)

6. Next, discuss the ways in which the syrup is not like a glacier. (It moves much faster; it doesn't have many wrinkles and crevasses; it doesn't change the terrain with its weight.)

FACT

Estimates suggest that there are 300,000 icebergs in the Southern Ocean at any given time.

EXTENSION ACTIVITIES

✳ Leave the materials at a learning center so that students can create, highlight, and experiment on their own "terrain."

✳ The Columbia glacier in Alaska travels about 20 meters (65 feet) per day on average. That's 7.3 kilometers (4.5 miles) per year! Pose this math challenge to the class: How far has the glacier traveled since students were born? If the glacier were on your playground, how far would it travel in the next week? in next month? during the school year?

WHEN ICE MEETS WATER

(science)

Materials   food coloring • ice cubes • clear containers

Antarctica is Earth's iceberg factory, creating 9 out of 10 icebergs. Icebergs are chunks of floating ice that may be small (called "growlers"), medium-sized (called "bergy bits"), or as large as Rhode Island. They break off from glaciers or ice sheets, the latter forming icebergs called tabular icebergs. These icebergs are flat on top and look like tables or thick slices of vanilla sheet cake.

During its life, an iceberg continuously breaks down, or melts into smaller and smaller bits until it finally disappears. Some start their lives trapped in pack ice, swirling in circles. Others bolt for the open sea. Most icebergs melt in or near the polar regions; a few have made it to temperate and even subtropical zones.

What happens when ice meets water? To demonstrate, make colored ice cubes using dark food coloring. Drop them into clear containers of water at various temperatures—very cold, room temperature, and very hot. As the ice cube melts, the denser cold water from the ice cube sinks, but also note the swirling patterns of the "currents." The water becomes more turbulent.

FACT

If Antarctica's ice melted, the world's sea level would rise 10 to 15 stories. Without its heavy shroud of ice, Antarctica would also rise above sea level, becoming a larger landmass.

EXTENSION ACTIVITY

In 1935, an arctic iceberg set a latitude record of 28°N.
In 1894, an antarctic iceberg made it to 26°S. What major cities are on or near these latitudes? Ask students to locate them on a map.

BOOK LINK

Ice, by Bernard Stonehouse (Macmillan Childrens' Group, 1992). Facts about a polar region's most plentiful natural resource.

SNOWFALL FIGHT

(reading a graph)

Materials Snowfall Fight reproducible (page 33) • almanac and other weather-reference materials • snow • straight-sided container • ruler

When people think of the poles, they usually think of snow and ice. But how much snow do the poles really get?

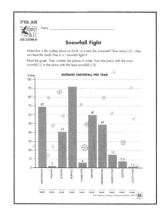

Begin a lesson on measuring snowfall by filling a straight-sided container with shaved ice or snow; measure the depth using a ruler. (Don't pack the snow.) Ask students to predict if the depth will increase, decrease, or stay the same after the snow melts. Challenge them to guess the post-melting measurement.

Results will vary depending on the density of the snow, but the water level can be dramatically lower. Ask students: Why did the level shrink so much? What made the snow take up more room? (Air pockets in the snow gave the snow more volume.)

Explain that for this reason, when meteorologists measure precipitation, they take into account the type of moisture that has fallen. Four inches of snow is no big deal; four inches of rain is a deluge. Each year, the Antarctic plateau receives about eight inches (about 20 cm) of snow, which is roughly the equivalent of two inches (5 cm) of rainfall.

FACT

In 1921, Silver Lake, Colorado got more snow in 24 hours than Antarctica gets in nine years!

The reproducible on page 33 asks students to rank the average annual snowfall of select places by placing the information on a graph. If necessary, guide them with such questions as: What does this graph show? (the average snowfall of certain places); How is average snowfall measured? (in inches); How many cities get more snow than Anchorage? (one—Buffalo); Which city gets about half as much snow as Buffalo? (Minneapolis)

When students are finished, discuss their results. Note that the North and South Poles are not the snowiest places on Earth—by far. In fact, the South Pole is the least snowiest, receiving about as much precipitation as the Sahara Desert.

EXTENSION ACTIVITY

How does the snowfall in your town or city compare with the places on the graph? (Note that most cities on the graph get rainfall in addition to the snowfall listed. Check an almanac for more complete climate data.)

POLAR THERMOMETER

(science)

Materials Polar Thermometer reproducible (page 34)

Meteorologists measure the temperature using the Celsius scale. In this activity, students can learn to become fluent in Celsius just as they became fluent in Fahrenheit—by associating temperatures with concrete experience.

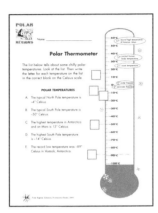

Begin by taking students up and down the Celsius scale. The key benchmark is 0°C (freezing point for water; just cold enough to snow). What would students wear at this temperature? (coat, hat, mittens, boots) Using 0° as a baseline, discuss what to wear as the temperature gets warmer: 10°C (jacket), 20°C (light sweater), 30°C (T-shirt and shorts), and 40°C (swimsuit). Then discuss what students would wear at colder temperatures: -10°C (coat, hat, mittens), -20°C (full winter wear), and -30°C (arctic survival gear)? (Students will become more familiar with the scale if you do not translate the degrees into Fahrenheit for them during this process.)

The final benchmark is 100°C—the boiling point of water. Anything between about 50°C and 100°C is hotter than any weather on Earth.

After students are comfortable with Celsius temperatures, copy and distribute the reproducible on page 34. Have students plot the temperatures on the thermometer.

EXTENSION ACTIVITY

On chart paper or other large paper, draw a Celsius thermometer for your classroom that ranges from -100° to 100°. Have students add polar temperatures to the thermometer and investigate other temperatures to add. They can use reference books, ask experts or family members, or do simple experiments to answer questions such as these:

JOKE

What do polar bears do on summer vacation?

They chill out!

What are the highest and lowest temperatures for your state?

What are the average seasonal temperatures for your state?

What is the highest fever you can remember having?

What is a comfortable temperature for your bath water?

How hot is a thermometer in the shade versus one in direct sun?

How cold are your freezer and refrigerator?

POLAR REGIONS

Group Number: _____

No Rain, No Drain

What happens to water when it melts on frozen ground? Try this experiment to find out. Your teacher will give you the materials you need.

PART I: Here's how to make an "earth pot."

1. Circle or write in the material you will use.

   soil   pebbles   sand   clay

   other _____

2. Put the two pots side by side. Fill them half full with your material.

3. Label one pot "W" for warm and the other "F" for freezing.

4. Write your group number on both pots.

5. Put the "F" pots in the freezer overnight. Keep the "W" pots at room temperature.

Group Number: _____

No Rain, No Drain

PART II: Test the pots for drainage.

1. How are the two pots different?

2. Put both of the pots in a pan. Add a spoonful of water to each pot. What do you observe?

3. How long will it take a half cup of water to drain through each pot? Will the water drain faster in one pot than in another? Record your prediction here

4. Pour a half cup of water in each pot. Time how long it takes to drain through the pots and out the bottom. Record the time.

   Pot W:

   Pot F:

POLAR REGIONS

Name: _____

Mile-High Ice

Suppose you could slice Antarctica like a cake. Your knife would cut the continent in two. You could see the layers from top to bottom. This diagram shows a slice of Antarctica. The land on the bottom is like the cake. The ice sheet on top is like the icing. Look at the diagram. Then answer the questions.

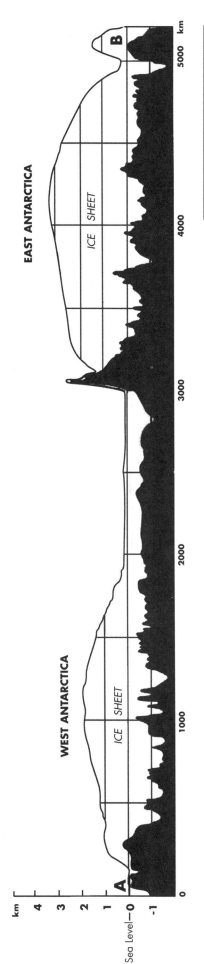

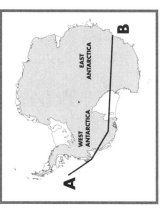

WEST ANTARCTICA

ICE SHEET

EAST ANTARCTICA

ICE SHEET

km
4
3
2
1
Sea Level—0
-1

0   1000   2000   3000   4000   5000   km

A

B

1. Write an "X" where Antarctica is highest.

2. Write a "Y" where the land is highest.

3. Is most of the land above or below sea level?

4. Look at the two ice sheets in the east and west. How would you describe their shape?

5. How would you describe the shape of the land?

Polar Regions Scholastic Professional Books, 2000

Name: _____

Glaciers Go With the Flow

Here comes a glacier! A glacier is a giant, frozen river. It flows at a "glacial" pace—very, very slowly.

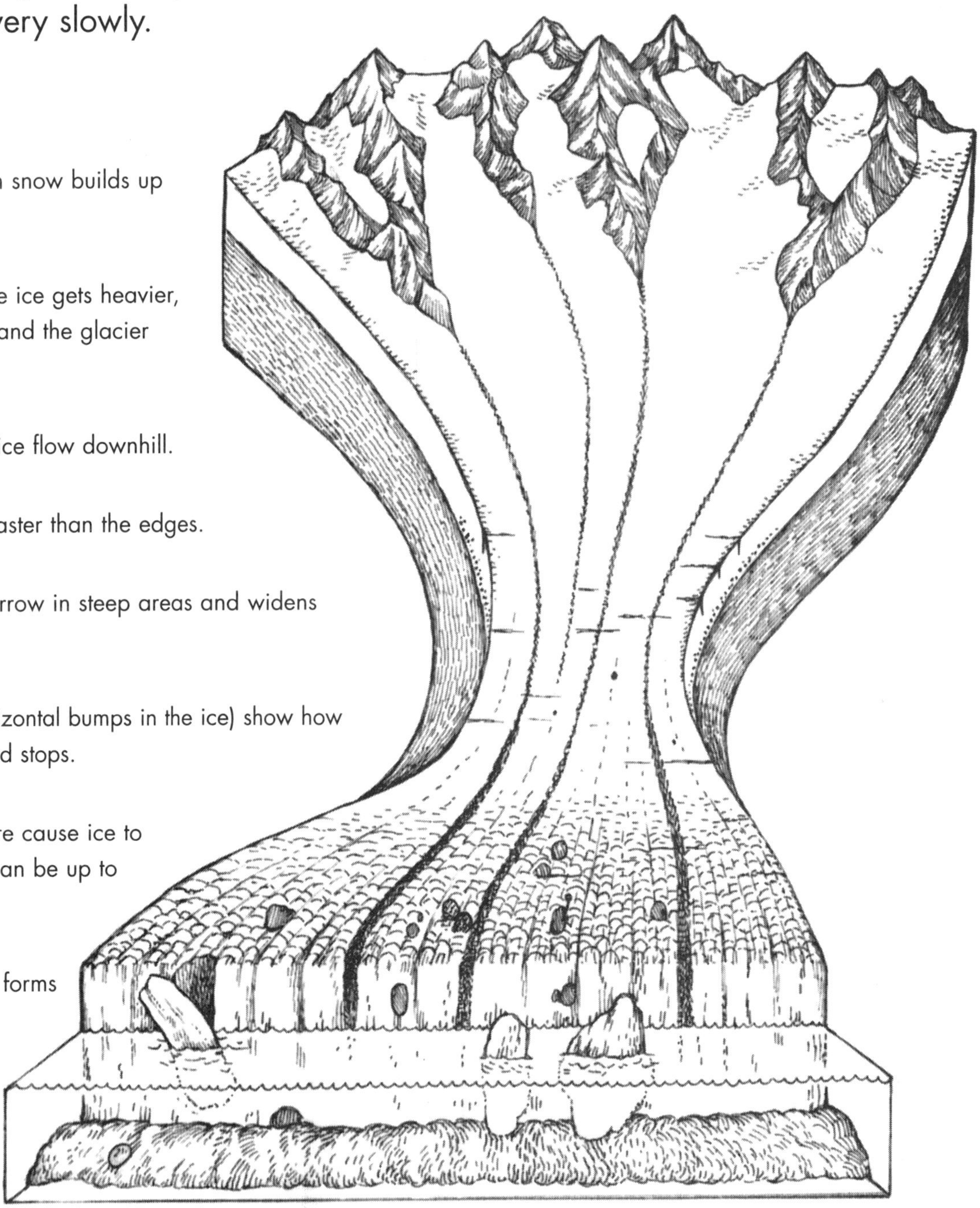

Glaciers form when snow builds up and turns to ice.

As the weight of the ice gets heavier, pressure builds up and the glacier begins to move.

Gravity makes the ice flow downhill.

The center travels faster than the edges.

The glacier gets narrow in steep areas and widens in flat areas.

Wrinkles (small horizontal bumps in the ice) show how the glacier starts and stops.

Motion and pressure cause ice to crack. The cracks can be up to 100 feet deep.

Tongue (wide part) forms at the front of the glacier.

Icebergs split off into the sea.

Name: _____

Snowfall Fight

Antarctica is the coldest place on Earth. Is it also the snowiest? How many U.S. cities can beat the South Pole in a "snowfall fight"?

Read the graph. Then number the places in order, from the place with the most snowfall (1) to the place with the least snowfall (10).

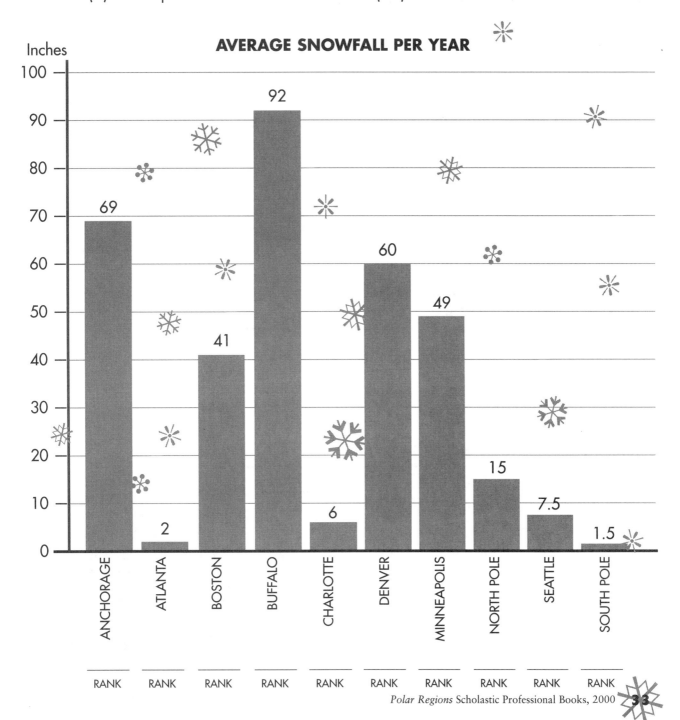

AVERAGE SNOWFALL PER YEAR

Inches

ANCHORAGE	69
ATLANTA	2
BOSTON	41
BUFFALO	92
CHARLOTTE	6
DENVER	60
MINNEAPOLIS	49
NORTH POLE	15
SEATTLE	7.5
SOUTH POLE	1.5

RANK   RANK   RANK   RANK   RANK   RANK   RANK   RANK   RANK   RANK

Name: _____

Polar Thermometer

The list below tells about some chilly polar temperatures. Look at the list. Then write the letter for each temperature on the list in the correct blank on the Celsius scale.

POLAR TEMPERATURES

A. The typical North Pole temperature is –4° Celsius.

B. The typical South Pole temperature is –50° Celsius.

C. The highest temperature in Antarctica and on Mars is 15° Celsius.

D. The highest South Pole temperature is –14° Celsius.

E. The record low temperature was –89° Celsius in Vostock, Antarctica.

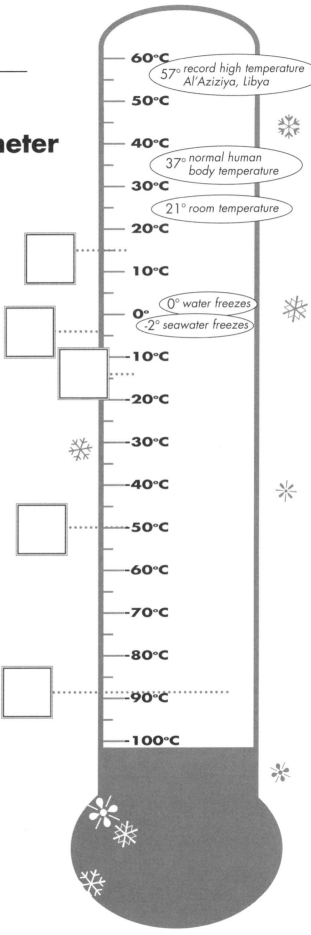

60°C — 57° record high temperature Al'Aziziya, Libya

50°C

40°C — 37° normal human body temperature

30°C — 21° room temperature

20°C

10°C

0° — 0° water freezes
        -2° seawater freezes

-10°C

-20°C

-30°C

-40°C

-50°C

-60°C

-70°C

-80°C

-90°C

-100°C

Polar Regions Scholastic Professional Books, 2000

SURVIVE AND THRIVE
ANIMAL AND PLANT ADAPTATION

Extreme climates call for extreme measures for survival. Few plants and animals can rise to the challenge, so polar ecosystems are among the simplest on Earth.

Polar Animals

Antarctica has no native land animals. In fact, it has very little exposed land—less than 2 percent of the continent is always free of ice. Tiny invertebrates arrived courtesy of sea-going animals. The largest, a wingless midge (a type of fly), is the size of a human-eye pupil in bright daylight. Antarctic creatures have many strategies for surviving including a chemical "anti-freeze" in their blood, the ability to be able to freeze and thaw without damaging their bodies, and the ability to go into a hibernation-like state so that they can exist without food for awhile. Humans have accidentally introduced snails, slugs, lice, and other creatures that are alien to Antarctica.

Antarctica's flora consists of hundreds of mosses, lichens, and other primitive plants that live in or on ice and rocks. In the seas surrounding the barren continent and on some sub-antarctic islands, simple food webs thrive.

The Arctic has a richer food web, especially on the tundra (the plain) and coastal regions. It is slightly warmer than Antarctica, and the land is connected to more hospitable and populated climate zones to the south. Even so, a healthy portion of arctic animals survive and thrive in the sea.

Coping with Cold

Polar animals cope with the climate in one or more of four basic ways:

- They hide by building dens or burrows (wolves, foxes, hares, polar bears).
- They travel or migrate to escape the worst of it (caribou and other reindeer, many sea birds).
- They are adapted to life in the sea, which is warmer and richer in food (seals, polar bears, walruses, penguins).
- They fight the frigid cold with defenses such as extra blubber and thick fur (musk oxen, seals, polar bears, whales, penguins).

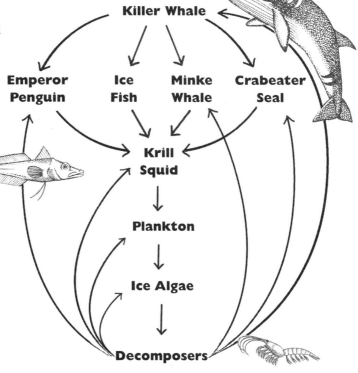

Killer Whale

Emperor Penguin   Ice Fish   Minke Whale   Crabeater Seal

Krill Squid

Plankton

Ice Algae

Decomposers

All of these survival strategies are either genetic (physical adaptations such as blubber and fur) or behavioral (migrating).

Only humans have a fifth choice: to use technology to change the environment. We do such things as build roads and cities, import energy and resources, and hook up electricity to survive. We'd succumb to polar conditions in minutes without these amenities. Our unclothed bodies are adapted to around 80°F (26°C) and so have few physical defenses. We don't have enough body hair to offer protection from the cold. Our limbs are long and gangly, allowing body heat to escape. Our methods of generating more body heat (shivering, for example) are inadequate. Our thin skin freezes easily.

Polar Plants

Unlike animals, polar plants can't easily migrate, burrow, or accumulate fat. But some arctic plants have adapted to the cold so they don't lose heat. Many grow low to the ground to avoid relentless winds. In the desert-like conditions, very shallow roots sop up surface moisture that can't penetrate permafrost. However, these same shallow roots can't stand up well to fierce winds.

How much abuse can a plant take? Compare Earth's most extreme trees—those nearest the northern tree line—to the trees in your region.

Subarctic trees, such as the larch and spruce, are much shorter, grow more slowly, and are more gnarled than their temperate cousins. They survive with half their branches, as arctic winds denude their windward side. The roots are precariously shallow

(extending less than 2 feet from the earth's surface), due to the hard permafrost. As water pools on the frozen plain, the shallow roots can "drown" from lack of oxygen.

The ranks of arctic trees very gradually turn sparse and then disappear. (A mountainous tree line is distinct and sudden.) The point at which they disappear is their threshold of life. North of this threshold, trees could tolerate the extreme cold and lack of light in winter, but the summer climate doesn't get warm enough (50°F or higher) for trees to grow. Trees must grow—even at a glacial pace—to survive.

ACTIVITIES

USING THE SURVIVE AND THRIVE CARDS

Cold is just one enemy to life in the Arctic and Antarctic. Animals must also cope with long, dark winters, extremely high winds, a very short summer, and sparse food and fresh water. The Survive and Thrive cards on pages 43-50 can help students understand the strategies that animals use to survive in these harsh conditions.

Many of the activities on these pages use the Survive and Thrive cards. To make the cards, reproduce the pages and cut out the cards. Fold each card in half along the dotted line and glue the front and back of the card together. Each card should have survival strategies on one side and an animal's picture and name on the other. For greater durability, glue the cards to pieces of cardboard or laminate the cards.

ANIMAL SURVIVAL STRATEGIES *(graphing)*

Materials   Survive and Thrive cards (pages 43 to 50) • bulletin board • index cards

1. Pass out one animal card per student (make a double set of cards for a large class). Give students time to read their cards. Then read aloud strategy 1 on the survival cards. Ask all "animals" who use this strategy to stand. (The strategy will be followed by the number 1 on their cards.) Count and record the animals that use this strategy.

2. Continue to count and record data for the rest of the strategies.

3. Make a class bar graph. Write each strategy number on an index card. Attach the cards in a vertical column on the bulletin board. This is the first column of your graph. Write the animal names on index cards and use your data to place the animal names in the correct row on the graph.

4. Use the graph to answer these questions:
  - Based on the nature of the strategies, what "enemies" do polar animals have to face? (cold, lack of food, predators, and so on)
  - Are any strategies common to almost all? (insulation)
  - Are any strategies unique (pertain to only one animal)?
  - Do most mammals share certain strategies? (dens, extra insulation)
  - Which strategies do birds share? (travel or migration, flocks)
  - How do the defenses of sea animals differ from the defenses of land animals?
  - How many strategies are genetic? How many are behavioral?

WHAT OTHER STRATEGIES?

(research)

Materials Survive and Thrive cards (pages 43 to 50)

The list of strategies doesn't include every survival mechanism of every animal on the cards.

For example, many arctic mammals grow up faster and become adults before winter sets in. Many whales and seals smash through ice from underneath to create breathing holes.

Some animals use certain strategies more than others. Musk ox get insulation from a double layer of fur (they don't migrate), whereas caribou fur is warm but not warm enough to protect them from extreme cold (they migrate). The cards highlight only the strategies that an animal relies on heavily or that are especially unique.

To further explore survival strategies, assign each student an animal card. Suggest that they research the animal's body parts, such as fins, legs, feet, tails, ears; the animal's blood circulation or the animal's body shape, to find out how they help the animal survive in the cold.

POLAR ANIMAL RESEARCH REPORT

(research)

Materials Polar Animal Worksheet (page 52) • encyclopedias and other books about polar regions and animals

Encourage students to add game cards to the Survive and Thrive set by researching additional animals. In the Antarctic, there are 17 varieties of penguins, several more types of seals and whales, many sea birds, and a rich population of invertebrates, such as the giant squid.

The Arctic has polar versions of many temperate animals. In fact, polar bears are modified brown bears. Suggest that students check out wolves, reindeer, seals and whales, the pika, the Arctic bee (it wears a fur coat and creates its own heat!), Dall sheep, ocean fish, and sea birds.

After students choose an animal to research, distribute page 52. Students can use the worksheet to record their findings. When they're finished, students can read their findings to the class. Invite students to turn their information into new strategy cards for the game.

SURVIVE AND THRIVE GAME

(science)

Materials Survive and Thrive Game reproducible (page 42) • Survive and Thrive Cards (pages 43 to 50) • Survive and Thrive Strategy Cards (page 51)

Assemble both the animal and strategy cards. Allow students to become familiar with the Survive and Thrive cards either by reading the cards on their own or by participating in some of the activities on pages 37 and 38. Then put the animal cards, the strategy cards, and the game rules on a table or at a learning center. Read the rules with students before playing, and discuss any questions they may have.

EXTENSION ACTIVITY

Many arctic animals have oversized feet, including arctic hares, arctic foxes, and polar bears. Caribou have split hooves that separate and spread out as the animal walks. These are examples of natural "snowshoes" that help the animal stay on top of the snow.

If a sandy or snowy area is available, have students explore how snowshoes work. (They spread the weight over a greater area, which means the foot doesn't press down as hard at any given point.) Students can make a series of tracks across the sand or snow: regular walking, on tip-toe, wearing oversized shoes, and even using short stilts! How deep do their tracks go? How do the different methods of walking feel?

JOKE

Knock knock.

Who's there?

Caribou.

Caribou who?

You don't have to cry about it!

BOOK LINKS

Antarctica: A Guide to the Wildlife, by Tony Soper (Bradt Publications, 1996). Encyclopedic descriptions of birds, mammals, fish and more.

"The Arctic World Series," which includes *Arctic Animals, The Arctic Land, Arctic Whales & Whaling, An Arctic Community,* all by Bobbie Kalman (Crabtree) is packed with information and photos.

PENGUIN PALS BULLETIN BOARD *(research, art)*

Materials Penguin Pal reproducible (page 53) • encyclopedias and other books about penguins

Perhaps no other polar animal has captivated our attention as much as the penguin has. How do these fascinating birds survive in the extreme cold of Antarctica? Use the reproducible on page 53 to explore this question—and others—with students.

Distribute the reproducible and have each child cut out his or her penguin. Challenge students to find one fascinating penguin fact and write it on the penguin. For a greater challenge, write penguin-related questions on slips on paper and have students each choose a question to answer. For example: What do penguins eat? How many different species of penguins are there? Or challenge students to research facts on a specific topic, such as how penguins stay warm or how they avoid predators. Students can also use the reproducible to record any fascinating polar facts they discover during the polar regions unit.

When all the penguin facts are filled in, display the penguins on a bulletin board or wall.

EXTENSION ACTIVITIES

✳ Challenge students to use the penguin template and crayons, markers, and paper scraps to make different species of penguins, such as the Adélie, chinstrap, Galapagos, yellow-eyed penguin, or king penguin.

✳ Copy the penguin template on white paper and cut out. Trace the shape on black construction paper; cut it out, and attach the two pieces so that one side is black and the other is white. Use this penguin to talk about how counter-shading keeps penguins safe from predators. Tape together a large white piece of paper (to represent ice) and a large dark-blue piece of paper (to represent the sea). Allow students to place the penguin in different places on the paper to see how counter-shading might work. Ask students: How might the penguin blend into the ice? (its white feathers are the same color, and a predator might not see it if it were looking at the penguin from the front.); How might a penguin blend into the sea? (the penguins dark feathers would be hard to see in the water, especially when the penguin is swimming and its belly is facing down); Do you think it's helpful for the penguin to have both colors? Why or why not? (answers will vary).

BOOK LINKS

Birds of Antarctica, by Lynn M. Stone, plus others in this Antarctica Series (Rourke, 1995).

Penguins at Home: Gentoos of Antarctica (1993) and *Summer Ice: Life Along the Antarctic Peninsula* (1995), by Bruce McMillan (Houghton Mifflin).

Playing with Penguins and Other Adventures in Antarctica, by Ann McGovern (Scholastic, 1995).

PLANTS GET TOUGH

(science)

Materials   Plants Get Tough reproducible (page 54) • fast-growing seeds such as radish, bean, alfalfa, or grass (or young seedlings) • empty Styrofoam egg cartons broken in half • potting soil • cookie sheets or other shallow pans

The polar regions are so harsh that any life-form, plant or animal, has to be very tough to live in them. The plants that live in the Arctic and Antarctic are special in this way.

Since students can't travel to polar regions, they can try growing plants under extra-tough conditions in the classroom.

To introduce the experiment, ask students: Could a plant survive in every nook and cranny of this room? Which places would be hard on a plant? Why? (places that lack light and heat, are too hot or cold, or are heavily trafficked) What conditions would make an ideal place for a plant to thrive? (moderate light, water, heat, and no disturbances)

Students can take home the reproducible and do the experiment independently or with parents. To do it as a class project, divide the class into groups of four and distribute a reproducible, half an egg carton, 6 seeds, and one to two cups of potting soil to each group. After planting the seeds in the egg cartoon, each group should choose a "Plant Zone" in your classroom (a tough place for plants to grow) and place the egg carton there. If you have access to a refrigerator, students may want to place one carton inside. Meanwhile, prepare a control egg carton and put it in an ideal plant location.

All of the egg cartons should receive the same amount of water—enough to keep the soil moist but not waterlogged. After germination, examine the results: How many of the six seeds sprouted in each egg carton? Graph the data and compare students' experimental plants with your control plant.

Remind students that seeds and plants need different things to survive. Seeds don't have leaves, so they don't make use of light the way plants do. All their food is stored inside the seed. Seeds can germinate in total darkness (some do better in darkness). They also prefer a cooler environment; your experiment may determine just how cool they can go. Seeds do need water, but waterlogged seeds probably won't germinate, due to lack of air.

EXTENSION ACTIVITY

How many plants continue to live? Have students keep a journal and make observations of the plants' development. This experiment can also be done with living plants instead of seeds.

The Survive and Thrive Game

Help three animals survive and thrive by matching them with the correct survival strategies.

GAME MATERIALS

1 set of Survive and Thrive animal cards • 2 sets of Survival Strategy cards
• Players: 2 to 6

SETTING UP

1. Spread out the animal cards picture side up.

2. Put the strategy cards facedown in a stack.

3. Each player draws one animal card and three strategy cards. Don't read your animal card! Place it picture side up in front of you.

4. The player with the latest birthday during the year goes first.

RULES FOR PLAYING

Your goal is to find three Survival Strategy cards that match the survival strategies on your animal card. When you find three, you can set your animal free. Set three animals free and you win!

1. TO TAKE A TURN: Read your three strategy cards. At each turn, you can either
   • Draw a new animal card. (Put the old one on the bottom of the deck) OR
   • Put one of your strategy cards on the bottom of a deck. Then draw a new strategy card.
   Do you think all three of your strategies match your animal? If not, your turn ends. If so, set your animal free (rule 2)!

2. TO SET YOUR ANIMAL FREE: Turn over the animal card. Look for the three numbers that match your three strategies.
   • If all three numbers match, congratulations! Your animal can survive and thrive. Put it in a safe place near you.
   • If a number is missing from the animal card, your animal can't survive. Put it on the bottom of the animal deck.
   • In either case, put your three strategy cards on the bottom of the deck. Draw a new animal card and three new strategy cards and wait for your next turn.

3. TO WIN: The first person to help three animals survive and thrive wins the game.

Survive and Thrive Animal Cards

Following the dashed line, cut out each card. Then fold in half along the dotted line and glue together.

POLAR BEAR

CARIBOU

MUSK OX

POLAR BEAR
Arctic Mammal

SIZE: Half a ton; at the shoulder, as tall as a 10-year-old human (3)

FOOD: Seals, beluga whales

BODY: Thick fur covers thicker blubber (1, 10). The fur looks white (14), but is clear. The skin is black (5). The feet are like sandpaper (11). Webbed toes help the polar bear swim (6). On their oversized paws (11), polar bears travel hundreds of miles for food (13).

BEHAVIOR: Mothers build a den (2). Most bears avoid humans (16).

CARIBOU (REINDEER)
Arctic Mammal

SIZE: A quarter ton; at the shoulder, as tall as an 8-year-old human (3)

FOOD: Willow, moss, lichen, grasses

BODY: The blubber is thick as a brick (1, 10) and the fur is warm as a blanket. Snowshoe-like hooves spread out to avoid sinking in snow (11). These dark reindeer (5) have thick bodies and short legs (4).

BEHAVIOR: Caribou migrate in giant herds (7, 9, 14, 15). They can even swim across rivers!

MUSK OX
Arctic Mammal

SIZE: A quarter ton; at the shoulder, as tall as an 8-year-old human (3)

FOOD: Moss, lichen, and other vegetation

BODY: The dark, thick outer hairs (5) are as long as a baseball bat (1)! The inner down fur is eight times warmer than sheep wool.

BEHAVIOR: Musk oxen huddle (8) to keep warm and for defense. Fur and blubber (10) allow these half-sheep, half-cattle to survive the winter instead of migrating. They can travel far to find food (13).

Survive and Thrive Animal Cards

SNOWY OWL

SNOWY OWL
Arctic Bird

SIZE: As heavy as a hamster; a wingspan about equal to the height of a 12-year-old human

FOOD: Hares, lemmings, smaller birds, fish, eggs (12)

BODY: This large owl (3) has feathers that even cover its beak (1)! They're snow white in winter and mixed in summer (14). This camouflage, plus extrasoft feathers, help the owls sneak up on prey.

BEHAVIOR: When food is scarce, they fly to southern Canada (13).

ARCTIC FOX

ARCTIC FOX
Arctic Mammal

SIZE: As heavy as a house cat; less than knee high at the shoulder

FOOD: Lemmings, hares, fish, polar bear leftovers (12)

BODY: The fur may be the thickest of all mammals (1). Even the soles of the feet have fur! The fur turns white in autumn and gray or blue in spring (14). The ears, legs, tail, and nose are short (4).

BEHAVIOR: They hide under the snow or ground (2). Their dens even have a built-in "freezer" for leftover food (10). Humans hunt foxes for their thick fur (16).

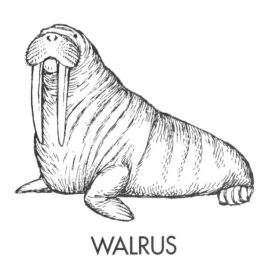

WALRUS

WALRUS
Arctic Mammal

SIZE: About a ton (more for males); when stretched, as tall as the rim of a basketball net (3)

FOOD: Clams, fish, and other sea creatures (6)

BODY: Thick blubber (1, 10) and skin (5) protect against the tusks of other walruses in fights. The compact bodies (4) have strong fins that double as legs on land (11). When warm, walruses circulate blood all over to cool off (9). When cold, they keep the warm blood deep inside.

BEHAVIOR: Walruses gather in the thousands (9, 15). In fall, they migrate (7, 13). Humans almost hunted walruses to extinction (16).

Survive and Thrive Animal Cards

ARCTIC (GRAY) WOLF

ARCTIC (GRAY) WOLF
Arctic Mammal

SIZE: As heavy as an adult woman; at the shoulder, as tall as a desk

FOOD: Caribou, hares, rodents, lemmings, fish, and more (12)

BODY: Some are light colored (14); others are dark (5) or mixed. Two layers of fur (1) and extra blood to the feet (9) keep them warmer.

BEHAVIOR: Wolves dig dens in the snow or ground (2). They travel alone or in packs to hunt (13). Most wolves avoid humans (16).

ARCTIC HARE

ARCTIC HARE
Arctic Mammal

SIZE: About the size and weight of a skinny house cat

FOOD: Arctic poppy, willow, and other vegetation

BODY: Winter white and autumn brown (14) Arctic hares are larger than their southern cousins (3). Their feet are extra large (11).

BEHAVIOR: Unlike other hares, they live in herds (15). If a wolf comes near, the whole herd takes off with a kangaroo-like hopping step (11). Hares fear almost every large animal— including human hunters (16). They burrow in snow (2).

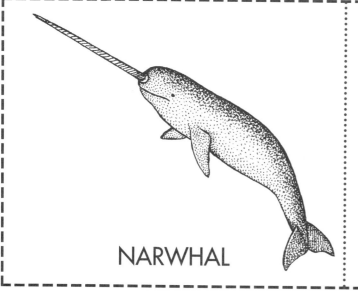

NARWHAL

NARWHAL
Arctic Mammal

SIZE: About a ton; as long as a small car (not including the tusk)

FOOD: Fish, squid, crustaceans (6)

BODY: These small whales look like plump unicorns (1, 4). Only the males have a single tusk, probably for fighting. The counter-shading (dark top, light bottom) helps to fool killer whales (14).

BEHAVIOR: Human hunters kill narwhals for skin, flesh, and tusks.

Survive and Thrive Animal Cards

COLLARED LEMMING

COLLARED LEMMING
Arctic Mammal

SIZE: About the size of a baseball, but half the weight

FOOD: Wildflowers, willows, other vegetation (12)

BODY: It has the thickest coat of any rodent (1). The fur changes from white (14) to brown (5) each season. The round shape and stubby limbs help keep in heat (4). Babies grow extra fast. They become adults before the short summer ends and winter arrives.

BEHAVIOR: They hide under the snow (2). In some years, there are dozens per acre (8,15); others, almost none. Lemmings migrate every few years (7).

ARCTIC TERN

ARCTIC TERN
Arctic/Antarctic Bird

SIZE: Lighter than two golf balls; a wingspan as wide as a standard door

FOOD: Fish, carrion (rotted food) (13)

BODY: The white body and black head blend in with icy terrain (14).

BEHAVIOR: The Arctic tern holds the long-distance record for migrating (7). It flies from North to South Pole and back again (13). Nesting sites house thousands of tern families (8, 15).

ORCA (KILLER WHALE)

ORCA (KILLER WHALE)
Arctic/Antarctic Mammal

SIZE: The length and weight of two average-size cars, placed bumper to bumper; dorsal (back) fin is as tall as a man (3)

FOOD: Almost anything that swims (6, 12)

BODY: Orcas are actually the largest dolphins (3), not whales. They have thick blubber (1, 10) and a sleek shape (4). Counter-shading may help orcas sneak up on prey (14).

BEHAVIOR: Orcas hunt in all four oceans (13). They tip over ice floes to get at seals! Pods of 30 to 45 whales cooperate to capture other prey (15).

Survive and Thrive Animal Cards

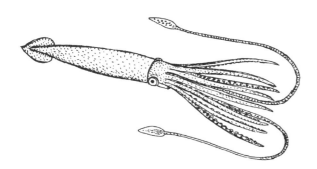

GIANT SQUID

GIANT SQUID
Arctic/Antarctic Invertebrate

SIZE: Half a ton; the body and tentacles can grow as long as three mini-vans (3)

FOOD: Fish, penguins, seals, and other seafood (6, 12)

BODY: The giant squid is the largest invertebrate (3).

BEHAVIOR: Many predators eat small squid. Only the sperm whale will tackle a giant squid. Giant squid live in waters from the northern Atlantic to the Southern Ocean (13).

HUMAN

HUMAN
Arctic/Antarctic Mammal

SIZE: Typical adults are about 5 to 6 feet tall and weigh 100 to 200 pounds.

FOOD: Variety of plants and animals (12)

BODY: Fat and fur can't fight polar cold. Stored fat can sustain a starving human for days (10). Human-made snowshoes, snowmobiles, and sleds cross thousands of miles of ice (11, 13).

BEHAVIOR: Humans build shelters (2). They wear thick clothing (1). Some migrate to warmer climates in winter (7).

EMPEROR PENGUIN

EMPEROR PENGUIN
Antarctic Bird

SIZE: As tall as a child in kindergarten, but twice as heavy (3)

FOOD: Fish, krill, squid (6)

BODY: A larger size, thick feathers (1), and a compact shape (4) hold in heat. Extra blood vessels keep feet from freezing (9). "Tuxedo" coat (5, 14) cloaks swimming penguins.

BEHAVIOR: Male emperors balance their egg on their feet. For two dark months, they huddle (8, 15) and live off stored fat (10). When the chick hatches, the female takes over. The thin, hungry males walk for hours or days to feed (13).

Survive and Thrive Animal Cards

ADÉLIE PENGUIN

ADÉLIE (AH DAY LAY) PENGUIN
Antarctic Bird

SIZE: As heavy as a 10-pound sack of flour; as tall as a hand towel is long

FOOD: Fish, krill, squid (6)

BODY: The "tuxedo" coat hides swimming penguins (5, 14). Adélies have thick feathers (1), a compact body (4), and great blood circulation (9) to keep in heat. Extra fat provides energy while parents hatch their eggs (10).

BEHAVIOR: Adélies toboggan down the ice on their bellies (11). They live in huge colonies (8, 15) and travel in winter (13).

WANDERING ALBATROSS

WANDERING ALBATROSS
Antarctic Bird

SIZE: As heavy as a large turkey; wingspan as wide as the key on a basketball court

FOOD: Squid, fish (6)

BODY: During its 50-year life span, a wandering albatross changes from dark brown (5) to totally white (14). It can fly thousands of miles (13) on long, strong wings.

BEHAVIOR: Albatrosses live full-time at sea. They sleep while floating on water or gliding in air. Since the birds follow ships, sailors can easily kill them for meat.

MINKE WHALE

MINKE (MINK EE) WHALE
Antarctic Mammal

SIZE: Six to eight tons (equal to about 4 cars); two car lengths long (3)

FOOD: Krill, squid, plankton (6)

BODY: Countershading (14) hides minkes from killer whales. Their sleek body helps them swim fast (4, 13). Like many whales, they have ample blubber (1, 10).

BEHAVIOR: Minkes migrate north in winter (7). They are curious about ships.

Survive and Thrive Animal Cards

KRILL

KRILL
Antarctic Crustacean (shelled invertebrate)

SIZE: As light as a paper clip; as long as a pinky finger

FOOD: Phytoplankton (6)

BODY: These shrimp-like creatures don't have much fat, yet somehow, they can survive half a year with-out eating (10). Krill are denser (heavier) than water. They would sink if they stopped swimming.

BEHAVIOR: Millions of tons of krill swarm near the surface (15). Almost every big predator in Antarctica eats them. But each krill lays 10,000 eggs at a time. Krill travel up and down and all around Antarctica for food (13).

SNOW PETREL

SNOW PETREL
Antarctic Bird

SIZE: Body as long as a ruler; wingspan almost as long as a yardstick

FOOD: Fish, squid, krill, plankton (6)

BODY: The snow-white feathers (14) blend with its pack-ice home.

BEHAVIOR: Snow petrels stick to their colonies (15). They dig nests in the snow or in cracks (2). If a predator approaches, the parents abandon the nest, leaving behind a foul-smelling oil to repel intruders. Some oil is 34,000 years old!

SOUTHERN ELEPHANT SEAL

SOUTHERN ELEPHANT SEAL
Antarctic Mammal

SIZE: Males weigh four tons, females just under 1 ton; males are as long as a small car, females a few feet shorter

FOOD: Squid (6)

BODY: The largest of all seals (3, 4) is dark (5) and has thick blubber (1, 10). It can dive more than half a mile down for 30 minutes. The milk of the females is half fat. Pups gain 20 pounds (9 kg) a day. Parents swim out to sea to feed (13).

BEHAVIOR: Elephant seals bask on the ice in large groups (15). Males puff up their elephant-like noses to attract females.

Survive and Thrive Animal Cards

ANTARCTIC FUR SEAL

ANTARCTIC FUR SEAL
Antarctic Mammal

SIZE: About the same as a typical pro-football player

FOOD: Fish, squid, krill (6)

BODY: These compact seals (4) have the thickest fur coats in the animal world (1). A bottom layer traps air. Outer hairs guard against the elements. Pups have a black coat (5). The fur seal's strong flippers can walk on ice (11). They have extra blood vessels (9).

BEHAVIOR: Fur seals live in groups (8, 15) and migrate (7).

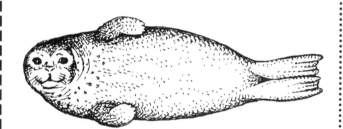

WEDDELL SEAL

WEDDELL SEAL
Antarctic Mammal

SIZE: Half a ton; as long as a basketball net is high

FOOD: Cod fish, crustaceans (shelled invertebrates), squid (6)

BODY: They have dark coats (5) and a white belly (14). Their build is compact (4) and blubbery (1, 10). Weddell seals can slow their breathing and heart rate. This allows them to stay underwater for up to an hour.

BEHAVIOR: These southernmost seals use their teeth to saw air holes in the ice. The seals communicate underwater by singing. The pups hang out together (8, 15), but their parents are loners.

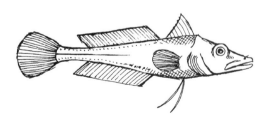

ICE FISH

ICE FISH
Antarctic Fish

SIZE: Long and thin like a baseball bat

FOOD: Krill, squid, plankton (6, 13)

BODY: The blood has no red blood cells. It's totally white! White blood is thin, so it flows faster and keeps the fish warmer (9). The blood also has a protein that keeps the blood (and the fish) from freezing. To get more oxygen, ice fish have bigger hearts that pump more blood.

BEHAVIOR: These predators swim (6) under the ice to hunt (13).

Survive and Thrive Game Cards

SURVIVAL STRATEGY 1

Extra insulation holds in body heat.

SURVIVAL STRATEGY 2

Burrows, dens, and snow caves are warmer.

SURVIVAL STRATEGY 3

A bigger size holds heat longer.

SURVIVAL STRATEGY 4

A compact shape (short limbs) reduces heat loss.

SURVIVAL STRATEGY 5

Dark colors absorb the sun's energy.

SURVIVAL STRATEGY 6

The sea is warmer and has more food.

SURVIVAL STRATEGY 7

Migrates to escape the harsh winter.

SURVIVAL STRATEGY 8

Huddles in large groups to keep warm.

SURVIVAL STRATEGY 9

Better blood circulation keeps body heat more constant.

SURVIVAL STRATEGY 10

Survives food shortages—by burning stored fat, for example.

SURVIVAL STRATEGY 11

Special feet can walk well on snow or ice.

SURVIVAL STRATEGY 12

Eats many foods—whatever comes along.

SURVIVAL STRATEGY 13

Travels far and wide for food.

SURVIVAL STRATEGY 14

Counter-shading or other camouflage helps to hunt or hide.

SURVIVAL STRATEGY 15

Large numbers are safer against predators.

SURVIVAL STRATEGY 16

Must be wary of humans (the top predator).

Name: _____

Polar Animal Worksheet

1. What is this animal called? _____

2. What kind of animal is it? (check one)

bird ☐   mammal ☐   insect ☐   fish ☐

other _____

3. Where does it live? _____

4. What does it eat? _____

5. Name one way it stays warm in cold weather. _____

_____

6. Name one way it protects itself from enemies. _____

_____

Draw a picture of it.

Name: _____

Penguin Pal

Write a fascinating fact on the penguin. Then cut out your penguin pal.

Name: _____

Plants Get Tough

Polar plants grow under tough conditions. This experiment will explore the toughest place a seed can sprout in your classroom.

MATERIALS

half an egg carton • potting soil • 6 seeds • pan • pen • notebook

PREDICTIONS

Where in the room would a plant have a tough time growing? Describe the spot.

_____

If you put a planted seed in that location, what do you think would happen? Would

the seed sprout? _____

PROCEDURE

1. Use a pen to poke one hole in the bottom of each egg case.

2. Fill each cup about halfway with soil.

3. Read the directions on your seed packet. Follow the directions to plant one seed in each cup.

4. Place your egg carton on a pan and put it in the tough location you've chosen.

5. Each day, check your seeds. Record any changes in your notebook. Keep the soil moist, but not soggy.

CONCLUSION

How many seeds sprouted? _____

Did your results match your predictions? _____

_____

What do you predict will happen to the seedlings? _____

_____

PEOPLE THEN AND NOW
HISTORY AND EXPLORATION

Polar People

Harsh conditions in Antarctica make it impossible for any humans to live there permanently. Explorers and scientists are the only people to brave this polar region. In contrast, the lands in the outer Arctic region are home to diverse people and a variety of cultures.

"Strait" to the Arctic

About 20,000 to 30,000 years ago, during the many ice ages, polar ice grew and melted over and over. When it grew, more seawater was locked up as ice and so sea levels fell, exposing a land bridge between Asia and North America. When the ice melted, sea levels rose again and covered the bridge. Thus, in fits and starts, animals and human hunters and settlers crossed the bridge into North America.

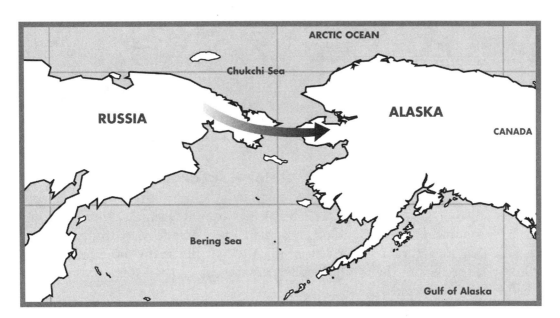

Arctic Peoples

Today, the Arctic is home to many groups of people, each with a distinct culture, language, and name. In Alaska, northern Canada, and Greenland, live bands of Inuit people. The word Inuit, which means "the people," is a general term that only applies to some bands. Eskimo, which means "meat eater," is considered derogatory by some bands, but is still widely used by others. Most Inuits prefer their specific cultural names, such as Karibou and Inupiaq.

North America is also home to other groups of native peoples, or Indians, such as the Dene. These Indian bands may have migrated over the Bering Strait earlier than Inuits; they settled areas south of the Arctic.

Other arctic peoples include the nomadic Lapps of northern Europe and Siberians, including a few Inuit bands, in Russia.

Because of their common polar environment, these diverse people share many of the same experiences. Familiar to them all are the nearly sunless winters, the brilliant northern lights, temperatures always below about 50°F (10°C), a traditional reliance on hunting and fishing, and art and artifacts made of animal parts, such as walrus ivory.

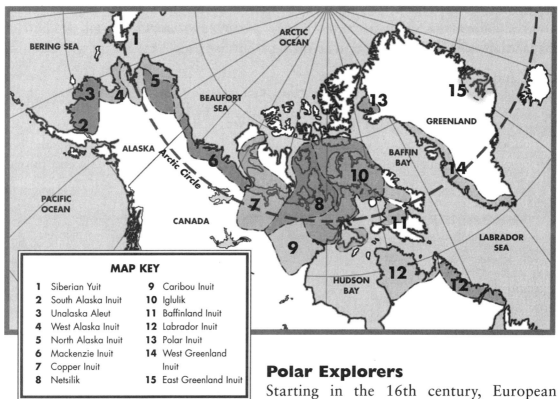

MAP KEY

1	Siberian Yuit	**9**	Caribou Inuit
2	South Alaska Inuit	**10**	Iglulik
3	Unalaska Aleut	**11**	Baffinland Inuit
4	West Alaska Inuit	**12**	Labrador Inuit
5	North Alaska Inuit	**13**	Polar Inuit
6	Mackenzie Inuit	**14**	West Greenland
7	Copper Inuit		Inuit
8	Netsilik	**15**	East Greenland Inuit

Polar Explorers

Starting in the 16th century, European explorers found their way to the Arctic. Henry Hudson, John Franklin, and others sought a faster trade route from west to east. Like these two adventurers, many died in the attempt. But many more followed. And like European settlers to the south, they left permanent marks—some of them scars—on the land and the people.

Since 1772, when James Cook embarked on the first expedition to find Antarctica, many explorers have also visited the South Pole. Today scientists work in this region for part of the year. The United States operates the Amundsen-Scott South Pole Station, which houses 120 people during the antarctic summer months.

Humans Survive and Thrive

One thing that native peoples, explorers, and scientists all have in common is that they have all found remarkable ways to survive in these harsh and dangerous regions. The activities in this section will explore the history and culture of arctic residents and explorers and also show students how people have devised clothing and shelter to protect themselves from the freezing temperatures.

ACTIVITIES

DOMED HOME OF SNOW *(science, math)*

Materials Domed Home of Snow reproducible (page 65) • eggshells cracked in half (a half shell per student with a few extras)

Traditionally, Inuits built igloos as temporary homes during the hunting season. Today's Inuits live, work, and go to school in modern buildings. A few central Inuit hunters still make igloos when traveling far from home. They can build these temporary shelters in an evening.

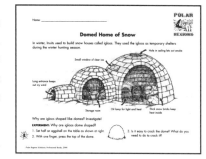

Copy and distribute the reproducible and ask students how an igloo is both similar to and different from a house. Ask students: Why do you think the igloos are dome shaped? After students make their guesses, have them perform the experiment using eggshells to test the strength of a dome.

Eggshells aren't perfect domes, but students will discover that their rounded ends are unbelievably strong. Make sure students press directly in the center of the "dome." Also, trim the bottoms of any shells that don't rest evenly on the table.

Explain that spheres and domes are the strongest shapes. Ask students to think about how a dome-shaped home might be useful in the snowy Arctic. (A dome-shaped home would resist breaking under the weight of heavy snow.)

EXTENSION ACTIVITIES

✳ How much weight can your eggshell domes withstand? Encourage students to experiment further by stacking books on top of four eggshell halves and recording their results.

✳ Have students research other traditional Inuit shelters, including half-buried sod houses (very energy efficient) and animal-skin tents (portable and easy to put up and take down). Inuit hunters used the tents in summer while they followed game. Challenge students to make models of different Inuit homes and display the models.

BOOK LINKS

Arctic Memories, by Normee Ekoomiak (Holt, 1988). In both his native tongue and English, a Canadian Inuk (singular of Inuit) describes his culture.

Houses of Snow, Skin, and Bones: Native Dwellings of the Far North, by Bonnie Shemie (Tundra Books, 1989). Inuits built tents, tepees, semi-underground houses, and stone sod houses.

MAKE AN INUKSHUK *(social studies, art)*

Materials   flat stones • modeling clay

An Inukshuk is an Inuit figure made of flat stones or slabs piled on top of one another to create a human form. The name Inukshuk is an Inuit word meaning "likeness of a

person" or "image of a man's spirit." An Inukshuk with arms outstretched might be found in northern Canada outside an Inuit home as a sign of hospitality. Other Inukshuk are used as markers or signposts to help guide Inuit across the treeless tundra.

Invite students to use flat stones or modeling clay to create their own Inukshuk for a classroom display. Inukshuk come in many forms and sizes, depending on what they are used for. If you have Internet access, search under the word Inukshuk to find many photos and drawings. Students can use these images to inform and inspire their own creations.

CARIBOU MAGIC *(language arts)*

Materials   Caribou Magic reproducible (page 66)

Photocopy the poem and distribute to students. First read the poem aloud, then invite students to read it a line at a time. Ask students: What is this poem about? The song, sung by an Inuit shaman (holy man) named Orpingalik, is a plea to the caribou to come around so that the singer can have soles for shoes and wicks for lamps. Some Inuit still rely in part on hunting and fishing for their food, clothing, and material for their artwork.

Ask students to think about what it might be like to hunt in the Arctic and then have them describe in writing what they see and hear

FACT

Caribou means "shoveler," because of the way caribou shovel away snow to find food.

and how they feel. Steer students to some of the books listed on page 57 to help inform their writing.

EXTENSION ACTIVITY

In Canada's Northwest Territories, a Native American tribe called the Dene hunt caribou for meat. The Dene found diamonds in the stomachs of the caribou, resulting in a "diamond rush" from as far away as Australia and South Africa. Discuss: What arguments would the Dene have against mining the diamonds? How might the miners respond?

WE SAY "SNOW"

(language arts, science)

Materials We Say "Snow" reproducible (page 67) • rocks, leaves, or other objects found in nature

At first thought, snow seems like snow—and nothing else. But Inuit languages recognize many facets of snow. Is it fallen or falling? pure or dirty? Has it shaped itself into a bank or other formation? Is it crunchy or soft?

The words on the reproducible are just a few of the many snow-related expressions of the Yup'ik Inuit of central Alaska. Pronunciation guides are impossible to provide, since many of the sounds don't exist in the English language. According to language expert Tony Woodbury of the University of Texas, the *c* is like *ch*, the *q* sounds Arabic, the *r* sounds Danish, the *e* is more like a short *u*, and the *vv* sounds like an *f*.

Keen observations and detailed descriptions of any natural object such as snow are useful in both creative writing and science. After students generate a word list on the reproducible, have them use it to write a poem or story.

Collect a variety of leaves, rocks, or other natural objects and ask students if they all look alike. Encourage them to describe the differences in detail. How many different descriptive words can students use? If they had to name a type of leaf or rock, what would they call it? Explain that scientists frequently name objects based on physical traits.

EXTENSION ACTIVITIES

❋ To test students' observation skills, ask each student to take an unshelled peanut (or an apple or an orange) from a bag. Students should study their peanuts very carefully. They should note unique features and draw a picture of them. Collect the peanuts, mix them, and put them on a table. Can each student pick out his or her peanut?

❋ The English language has adopted many Inuit words: igloo (or iglu), umiak (large, open boat), kayak, pemmican (high energy meat bar), mukluks (boots), parka (hooded winter jacket). Give students the words and have them provide you with definitions. Do they notice any patterns in the words? (The words are specific to Inuit life; the objects didn't exist in Western culture.)

FACT

Inuit languages are rich in words for animals and hunting, but they have only one word for "wildflower" despite the many Arctic species. There are no native swear words.

POLAR PARLOR GAME *(history, research)*

Materials Polar Parlor Game cards (pages 68 and 69) • reference materials

The "Polar Parlor Game" is a fun way for students to test what they've learned about polar explorers.

To prepare the class for the game, assign each student one of the explorers named on the reproducible game cards. Challenge each student to research the explorer on the card and present a short report to the class. Students may use encyclopedias, nonfiction books, news clippings, and the Internet to learn about the explorers.

When students are familiar with the explorers, photocopy the cards and mount them on cardboard. Laminate the cards if possible. Then divide the class into groups of three. At random and in secret, give each student a role card. Students ask questions of their two partners in order to deduce their identities. They also field questions from partners without revealing their own name.

Encourage students to ask questions such as: What country are you from? What is your main claim to fame? What type of transportation did you use? When necessary, players can answer, "I don't know" or "I'm not sure." Listen for unknown answers or factual mistakes to discuss afterward.

After a few minutes, students must guess the names of the two other people in their group. They score one point for every correct guess. When the first round is over, collect the role cards, redistribute them at random, and play another round.

EXTENSION ACTIVITIES

✳ Add polar figures other than explorers, including an Inuk hunter, a dog musher, a scientist, a tourist, and so on, to the game.

✳ Paste the role cards on larger index cards and invite students to add more facts to each card.

✳ Have the entire class play together. You could even stage a "masked ball" with paper masks to create an atmosphere of mystery!

✳ Play the game with polar animal cards (see the Survive and Thrive cards on pages 43-50). Students could ask such questions as, What do you do when winter comes? Who's your biggest enemy? What color are you? What do you eat?

BOOK LINKS *Arctic Hunter*, by Diane Hoyt-Goldsmith (Holiday House, 1994). The title subject is a ten-year-old Inuit boy named Reggie, who moves back and forth between traditional and modern worlds.

The Falcon Bow: An Arctic Legend, and other titles, by James Houston (Macmillan, 1986).

In a Different Light: Growing Up in Yup'ik Eskimo Village in Alaska, by Carolyn Meyer (Simon & Schuster, 1996). Fictional family exemplifies changes in the culture.

90° SOUTH OR BUST!

(geography, history, reading a diagram)

Materials   90° or Bust! reproducible (page 70)

Many explorers—all of them men and almost all of them European—have attempted to set latitude records near and on Antarctica. The "race to the Pole" lasted from Cook's 1772 circumnavigation of Antarctica to Amundsen's successful South Pole conquest in 1911.

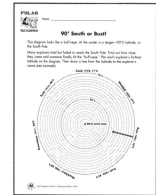

The diagram gives some idea of how tough it was to reach the South Pole. Expedition after expedition was turned away by weather, accidents, low provisions, inexperienced mistakes, and deadly ice. Shackleton was just 180 km (112 miles) from the South Pole when he was forced to turn back! He never reached his goal.

After students have finished their diagrams, ask them to describe any interesting patterns. Ask students: Who "won" the race? (Amundsen.) Were the attempts at reaching the pole evenly spaced in time or bunched up? (bunched up) At what time was polar exploration at a peak? (early 1900s.) When was racing to the South Pole less important? (last half of the 19th century.)

Many sealing and whaling captains probably beat the earlier records. But their main goal was hunting, not fame and fortune. They didn't publicize their latitude records. Do students think records are important? Ask them to think about the other types of records we honor (such as Guinness Book records and sports, CD sales, and academic records). How did the explorers' feats change our lives? What if no one had ever visited Antarctica? or ventured into the Wild West? or blasted into orbit?

EXTENSION ACTIVITY

Have students investigate records for Antarctica:

- Captain James Cook came close to Antarctica in 1772, but Fabian von Bellingshausen of Russia was probably the first to spot the continent (from 69°S) in 1820.

- Dumont D'Urville of France landed on Antarctica, possibly after sealers had, in 1840.

- James Ross named Antarctica's mountains Erebus and Terror, after his ships, which later took Sir John Franklin on his ill-fated arctic voyage; Ross was the first to climb the mountains in 1841.

- Adrien de Gerlache of Belgium got stuck in pack ice and so by default became the first to overwinter on the Antarctic continent in 1898; his experience proved that humans could set up bases there.

- Admiral Byrd of America was the first to fly over the South Pole in 1929; today, cargo planes play a vital role in keeping residents of Antarctica alive.

SCOTT'S LAST MESSAGE *(reading, writing)*

Materials Scott's Last Message reproducible (page 71)

In 1910, Captain Robert Falcon Scott of Britain and his team of explorers set out to become the first to reach the South Pole. Scott and his team were in a race with Norwegian explorer Roald Amundsen. Although Scott reached the Pole on January 17, 1912 he was too late. Amundsen not only won the race, but he made it home alive. Scott and his team were not so lucky. They died on the trip home.

As Scott lay dying in a tent, he wrote a gallant message to the people of Britain. His last words were was both an explanation of what went wrong and a plea for others to remember his companions with honor and to take care of their families.

Introduce Scott's story and ask students what might go wrong on a polar exploration. What are the dangers? Which dangers can an explorer control or avert? Which ones are just sheer bad luck?

The harsh climate and remote setting leave almost no margin for error. Here's what Scott believed went wrong with his mission:

- the use of ill-suited ponies, which died
- severe weather, even by antarctic standards
- soft snow, which slowed them down
- low supplies due to too many delays
- the accidental death of the strongest member in the group
- the illness of another group member

Distribute the reproducible for students to read. Discuss the concept of good risk and bad risk. Scott took a risk that something bad (death) might happen, so that something good (being the first to the Pole) might happen. Debate: Is reaching the Pole worth risking your life? Compare Scott's risky choice to that of astronauts, race car drivers, workers in a chemical factory, and airplane pilots.

After your discussion, have students write a personal-response essay to Scott's message.

BOOK LINKS

Iditarod Dream: Dusty and His Sled Dogs Compete in Alaska's Junior Iditarod, by Ted Wood (Walker, 1996). Dusty is a 15-year-old Alaskan musher. The junior race is a grueling 158 miles.

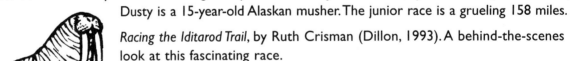

Racing the Iditarod Trail, by Ruth Crisman (Dillon, 1993). A behind-the-scenes look at this fascinating race.

Dogsong (Bradbury Press; 1985), *Woodsong* (Bradbury Press, 1990), and *Dogteam* (Delacorte Press; 1993), by Gary Paulsen. The acclaimed young-adult writer captures the art of dog sledding in both nonfiction (*Woodsong*) and fiction.

RACE THE IDITAROD! *(reading a map)*

Materials Race the Iditarod! reproducible (page 72)

The 1,100-mile Iditarod Trail Sled Dog Race zigs, zags, climbs, and drops from Anchorage to Nome, in Alaska. Some mushers get lost by following false trails.

Distribute and discuss the Iditarod Trail map. Before students answer the questions, review map-reading skills by asking volunteers to answer or point out the following: What does this map show? How does the map show bodies of water? Which line on the map shows the Iditarod trail? What symbol on the map shows an Iditarod checkpoint?

EXTENSION ACTIVITIES

✳ Students can investigate the history of the Iditarod or the science and sport of sled dogs (how they survive the cold while sleeping outside, how fast they can go, how much they can pull, etc.).

✳ Have students secretly choose a landmark somewhere on school grounds. The landmark could be anything—a swing, a vending machine, a poster. The challenge is to draw a map from the classroom to this location, including as much detail as they feel is necessary. Have students exchange their maps and try to find each others' landmarks.

SURVIVAL SUITS: YESTERDAY AND TODAY *(science)*

Materials Survival Suits: Yesterday and Today reproducible (page 73)

Northern people use heaters and fires to stay warm in winter. But if they didn't have either heat source, how could they stay warm? Have students ever felt really, really cold? What did they do about it?

Copy and hand out page 73 to students. Together look at the diagram, which shows how traditional Inuit peoples dress to protect themselves from the cold. Direct students to cut and paste the labels into their proper place on the diagram.

Discuss the Inuit survival gear. Ask students: Why do you think Inuits used so many animal skins? (in the Arctic, they didn't have easy access to cotton, linen, and other plant-derived cloths; game was plentiful)

EXTENSION ACTIVITY

Have students find pictures of modern survival gear in books and magazines. Copy the pictures and challenge students to create labels for them based on their research. As a class, compare and contrast the modern gear with the traditional Inuit gear.

FACT

Parkas and other clothes sometimes froze stiff. Inuits beat their clothes every day to soften them up. Some chewed on the leather for the same reason.

SURVIVING IN THE WILD *(science)*

Materials Surviving in the Wild reproducible (page 74)

In his book *Winterdance*, Gary Paulsen describes cold at sunset in Alaska: "Then it became dark. And the bottom dropped out. Cold came at me from everywhere. Any seam, any crack, any opening and I could feel jets of it, needles of it, deadly cutting edges of ice, worse than ice, absolute cold coming in."

Do students think they could survive in a polar region? Copy and distribute page 74 and have students take the quiz to find out. Then discuss the answers:

1. Dressing: Loose boots (and socks) allow blood to circulate. Blood acts like a heat exchanger as it runs through the body. It takes away some of the cold from toes and leaves behind some of its warmth. Multiple layers allow air to circulate (air traps heat inside) and also allows the wearer to remove a layer when overheated or sweating. Rescuers can spot bright colors more easily.

2. Storms: In any cold-weather situation, sleeping or staying still can be deadly. Moving the muscles makes them "fire" and create heat. That's why muscles shiver when you get cold. Do everything you can to stay warm—including starting a fire. In some cases, it's the only hope. A compass is useless in the Arctic. The Arctic has no trees or small trees. Snow has pockets of air that help insulate.

3. Frigid water: Clothes help you stay afloat. Plus, you only have a few seconds to stay alert in frigid water. Spend every one of them getting to dry ground. Swim and kick your feet to keep blood circulating. Grabbing a cold, metal pole with a bare (or gloved), wet hand will make the two instantly freeze together. Never touch cold metal with bare flesh.

FACT

Mittens keep you warmer than gloves. They have less area exposed to the air.

4. Running: Shallow breaths will keep your lungs from freezing (and so will a face mask). Goggles are vital to reduce glare and prevent snow blindness. Believe it or not, underdressing is better than overdressing. You can easily add layers, but overdressing causes the body to sweat more, and even removing layers won't keep a wet body from feeling cold.

BOOK LINKS *Julie of the Wolves,* by Jean Craighead George (Harper & Row, 1972). A girl survives alone in the Arctic without her family.

Shivers and Goose Bumps: How We Keep Warm, by Franklyn M. Branley (Thomas R. Crowell, 1984). The physics of heat, Inuit architecture, solar houses, animal adaptations, and cold-weather survival clothing for upper-elementary readers.

Toughboy and Sister, by Kirkpatrick Hill (Margaret McElderry, 1990). An 11-year-old boy and his sister try to survive in the Alaskan wilderness after their father disappears.

Name: _____

Domed Home of Snow

In winter, Inuits used to build snow houses called igloos. They used the igloos as temporary shelters during the winter hunting season.

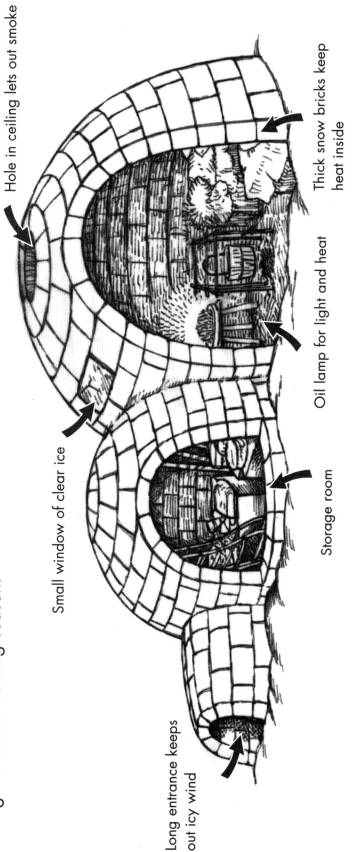

Hole in ceiling lets out smoke

Thick snow bricks keep heat inside

Small window of clear ice

Oil lamp for light and heat

Storage room

Long entrance keeps out icy wind

Why are igloos shaped like domes? Investigate!

EXPERIMENT: Why are igloos dome shaped?

1. Set half an eggshell on the table as shown at right.

2. With one finger, press the top of the dome.

3. Is it easy to crack the dome? What do you need to do to crack it?

 65

Name: _____

Caribou Magic

Wild Caribou, land louse, long-legs,

With the great ears,

And the rough hairs on your neck,

Flee not from me.

Here I bring skins for soles,

Here I bring moss for wicks,

Just come gladly

Hither to me, hither to me.

—*Song by Orpingalik*

caribou (KARE ih boo):
 a type of deer

louse: tiny insect that lives
 off other animals

wick: like the wick in a
 candle, moss burns
 slowly in an oil lamp

WRITE ABOUT IT

What might it be like to be an arctic hunter? On the back of this paper, write a paragraph describing what you see and hear, and how you feel.

Name: _____

We Say "Snow"

We say "snow." The Inuits of central Alaska say…

QANUK: snowflake

QANIR-: to snow

KANEQ: frost

KANEVVLUK: snow mixed with rain

NATQUIK: drifting snow

NAVCAQ: snow about to collapse

NEVLUK: snow with debris in it

ANIU: snow on the ground

MURUANEQ: soft, deep snow

QETRAR-: for snow to form a crust

NUTARYUK: fresh snow

UTVAK: block of snow

QENGARUK: snow bank

WRITE ABOUT IT

Think of the word snow. Think about how it feels (or how you imagine it feels). Think about how it looks. What other words does the word snow make you think of? List as many as you can on the back of this paper. Then use the words in a story or a poem.

Polar Parlor Game Role Cards

EXPLORER

ERIC THE RED

(late 10th century) Viking or Norseman

* Founded the first colony on Greenland

* Son Leif Ericson explored northern North America

* His red hair and beard earned him his nickname

EXPLORER

HENRY HUDSON

(? – 1611) Britain

* In 1610, explored namesake Hudson Bay in search of a Northwest Passage to the Pacific

* Sailed the Hudson River for the first time in 1609

* Left adrift to die with son and crew, but mutineers were later killed by Inuits or put in prison

---

EXPLORER

JOHN FRANKLIN

(1786 – 1847) Britain

* Vanished while seeking the Northwest Passage; rescue ships searched for years

* Final expedition consisted of two ships, the Erebus and Terror

* Bodies of crew were not found until 1859

EXPLORER

ROBERT E. PEARY

(1856 – 1920) United States

* In 1909, after 18 years of trying, was first to reach the North Pole

* Learned and used Inuit ways of surviving; four Inuits joined him at the Pole

* Was made a Rear Admiral in 1911 as a result of his achievement

---

EXPLORER

MATTHEW HENSON

(1866 – 1955) United States

* A sharecropper's son, he became a sailor at age 12

* Joined all of Robert Peary's arctic expeditions

* Learned Inuit language and became an excellent musher (dog sledder)

EXPLORER

LOUISE ARNER BOYD

(1887–1972) United States

* Born in San Rafael, California

* Led science expeditions to the Arctic; photographed unexplored lands

* Landed on northernmost point of Greenland; first woman to fly over North Pole

Polar Parlor Game Role Cards

EXPLORER

RICHARD BYRD

(1888 – 1957) United States

* Claimed to be the first to fly over North Pole

* In 1929, became first to fly over the South Pole

* Led the largest Antarctic expedition in history in 1947

EXPLORER

ANN BANCROFT

(1956 –) United States

* Taught school in Minnesota.

* One of only a handful of humans (and the only woman) to travel by dog sled to both poles

* The 1986 North Pole expedition was the first dog-sled trip since Robert Peary's famous feat in 1909

EXPLORER

JAMES COOK

(1728 – 1779) Britain

* Led three great voyages of discovery in the southern hemisphere

* In 1772, circled Antarctica without seeing it, but crossed the Antarctic Circle

* Reached the Hawaiian Islands in 1778

EXPLORER

SIR ERNEST SHACKLETON

(1874 – 1922) Britain

* Accompanied Captain Scott on the National Antarctic Expedition (1901-1904)

* His photographer took excellent photos and made films of Antarctica.

* Ice crushed his ship, which sank, but whole crew survived.

EXPLORER

ROBERT F. SCOTT

(1868 – 1912) Britain

* Led the National Antarctic Expedition (1901-1904)

* In 1902, made the first flight in Antarctica (in a balloon).

* In 1912, was second to reach the South Pole, but died on return trip.

EXPLORER

ROALD AMUNDSEN

(1872 – 1928) Norway

* In 1911, became first to reach the South Pole

* Used Arctic sled dogs and skis in Antarctica

* Flew over the North Pole in 1926

90° South or Bust!

This diagram looks like a bull's-eye. At the center is a target—90°S latitude, or the South Pole.

Many explorers tried but failed to reach the South Pole. Find out how close they came until someone finally hit the "bull's-eye." Plot each explorer's farthest latitude on the diagram. Then draw a line from the latitude to the explorer's name (see example).

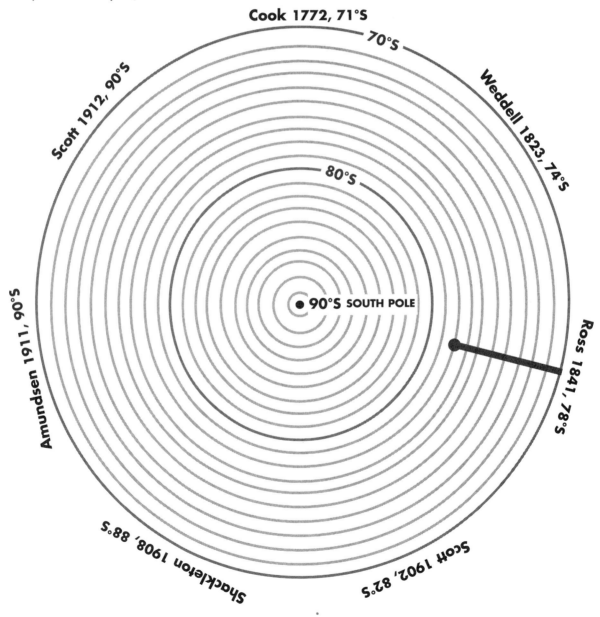

Polar Regions Scholastic Professional Books, 2000

Name: _____

Scott's Last Message

Captain Robert Scott's group was not the first to reach the South Pole. Just one month before them, explorer Roald Amundsen had beat them. Deflated, Scott's group headed home. As supplies ran low, a storm pinned them inside their tents. They were just 11 miles from One Ton Camp, a supply depot.

These are Captain Scott's last words:

> For four days we have been unable to leave the tent—the gale howling about us. We are weak. Writing is difficult. But for my own sake, I do not regret this journey…
>
> We took risks. We knew we took them. Things have come out against us. And therefore we have no cause for complaint, bow to the will of Providence, determined still to do our best to the last…
>
> Had we lived, I should have had a tale to tell of the hardihood, endurance, and courage of my companions…
>
> These rough notes and our dead bodies must tell the tale. But surely, surely, a great rich country like ours [Britain] will see that those who are dependent on us are properly provided for.

—*Robert Falcon Scott, March 23, 1912*

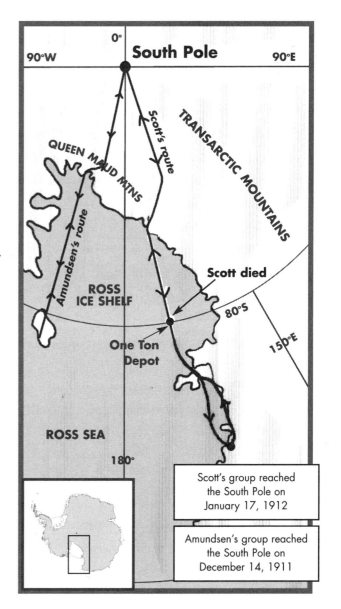

Scott's group reached the South Pole on January 17, 1912

Amundsen's group reached the South Pole on December 14, 1911

Name: _____

Race the Iditarod!

Look at the map and answer the questions below.

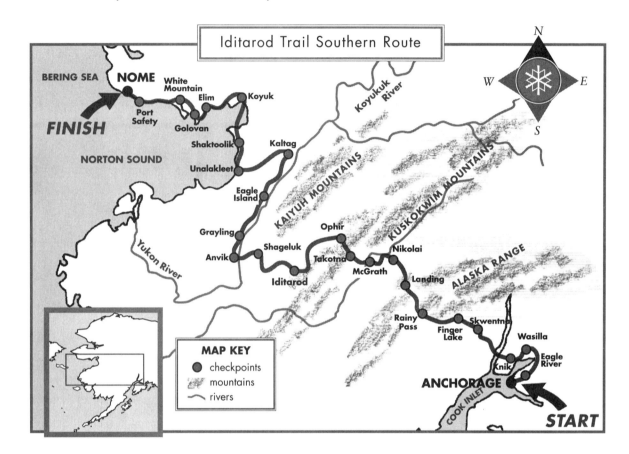

QUESTIONS

1. In what city does the dog-sled race start? _____

2. In what city does it end? _____

3. In what compass direction does the course generally go? _____

4. Checkpoints from Nikolai to Ophir are close together. Why can't mushers travel as far in this area? _____

5. Why doesn't the trail go in a straight line? _____

POLAR REGIONS

Name: _____

Survival Suits: Yesterday and Today

What did traditional Inuits wear to stay warm in the extreme cold? Look at this picture of a woman wearing traditional Inuit clothing. Cut out the labels at the bottom of the page. Then paste each label in the correct spot.

Wood sunglasses block glare from snow.

Women wore leather tunics and pants.

The parka is mostly Arctic ground squirrel.

The sleeves have trim made of red fox.

Mukluks (animal-skin boots) kept feet warm and comfortable.

Layers of light bird skins under the parka let air in and sweat out.

Wolverine and beaver fur around the hood keeps wind and snow off the face.

Gloves are lined with fur, which has air pockets for added warmth.

Name: _____

Surviving in the Wild

Could you survive polar weather? Read each event. Then circle the best choices for the items listed.

1. You're getting dressed for a winter day in the Arctic.

wear tight boots OR wear loose boots?

wear one heavy coat OR wear three or four layers?

stay bundled up OR remove clothing when you sweat?

choose bright colors OR stick with basic white?

2. You get lost in a storm.

shiver and stomp your feet OR try to stay still?

use a compass OR wait out the storm and use the stars?

build a snow shelter OR find a tree for shelter?

try to start a fire or stove OR don't bother

3. You fall through ice into frigid water.

remove clothes OR keep on clothes?

keep moving OR stay still?

wait for help OR try to climb out?

grab a cold metal pole OR grab a wooden pole?

4. You're running on a sunny, very cold day.

breathe deeply OR take short, shallow breaths?

wear goggles OR keep your eyes clear and free?

underdress OR overdress?

keep your body dry OR let sweat cool you off

CULMINATING ACTIVITIES AND GAMES
REVIEW AND EXTEND

Reprise the Mental Map Activity
Redo the mental map activity from the beginning of the unit (page 6) and compare students' level of detail and accuracy. You could also have students imagine and compare mental maps of the North Pole and South Pole. What facts did students find most surprising about the polar regions?

Sing a Song
Write the words to an Antarctica anthem, set to the music of "America the Beautiful" or to a rap beat. The words should capture the essence of the place and make it sound inviting to visit.

Global Awareness
The North and South poles are on exact opposite sides of the globe. What geographic feature is directly opposite your area? Have students use a globe to figure out how to solve this problem on their own. Encourage them to look for a pattern or rule that makes this challenge easier. They may discover that the latitudes of two opposite places are the same, but one is north and the other is south. The longitudes east and west add up to 180. For example, Hawaii is just south of the Tropic of Cancer at roughly 20°N 155°W. Its opposite is just above the Tropic of Capricorn at 20°S 25°E—Namibia, Africa.

Polar Timeline
Create a timeline of arctic events, including settlements, explorers, and modernization.

Get On-Line
E-mail Inuit children at an elementary school. Search for their web sites by using the words Inuit and elementary or by following the links from Internet addresses listed in the resources on pages 78 and 79. Exchange artwork, weather data, local recipes, and your class's "top 10" list for music or other popular culture.

Figure Fun
Mold Inuit figurines (polar bears, seals, and other animals are popular)

out of white modeling clay. Carving figures out of Ivory soap is tougher, but can be simplified. First, draw a figure on paper the same size as the soap. Tape the paper to the soap and trace over the lines of the design with a pen or pencil, creating an impression in the soap. Remove the drawing and carve the soap around the impression. Use a pencil to add details.

Be a Polar Reporter
Create an "Arctic News" newspaper that includes articles about an Inuit village, the Iditarod dog race, celebrations or holidays, an opinion piece about an important issue, a weather report, and maps and drawings.

Let It Snow
If you live in a snowy climate, investigate various types of snow and how it relates to the weather conditions (temperature, humidity, wind speed). Snow observations could include

wetness (good or bad snowball packing)

heaviness or density

powderiness (what happens when you blow on it?)

crunchiness (how much noise does it make when you walk on it?)

crustiness or ice content

purity

melting point (related to purity)

Icy Does It
Stage an ice-melting contest. Students can freeze a cup of water in any shape they like. Use various paper cups and plastic containers. The goal is to find a shape that will melt the slowest—generally the shape with the least amount of surface area— and the fastest. A sphere has the least amount of surface area for its volume.

Polar Brochures
Have students write and illustrate travel brochures for the North or South Pole. What activities will the tour include? What exciting features will vacationers see?

USING THE POSTER

Throughout your polar regions unit, students will discover how Antarctica and the Arctic are different from each other. The poster will provide students with an overview of the polar regions and allow them to make comparisons between the two areas.

Here are some suggestions for using the poster:

✳ Before beginning a study of the polar regions, hang the poster in your classroom to give students a preview of the material you will be covering. Make the poster the centerpiece of a Polar Regions learning center.

✳ Invite students to use the poster as a source of possible research ideas. Students can select any of the people, places, and animals featured on the poster and investigate the subject further. For example, students might want to find out more about the Amundesn-Scott station at the South Pole, the polar ice pack, or arctic terns. Students can share their research with the class in short presentation or in a written report.

✳ To wrap-up a unit on the polar regions, challenge students to create their own Polar Regions posters. Students can work in small groups to create posters that summarize what they have learned about both the Arctic and Antarctica. The posters can feature photos they have found in magazines or students' illustrations, along with brief descriptions. The posters might focus on a specific topic, such as animals, terrain, or plants, or capture all the elements of the North and South Poles.

POLAR RESOURCES

Books for Teachers

Antarctica: Travel Survival Kit (Lonely Planet, 1996).

Crossroads of the Continent: Cultures of Siberia and Alaska, by William W. Fitzhugh and Aron Crowell (Smithsonian, 1988).

The Ice: A Journey to Antarctica, by Stephen J. Pyne (Ballantine, 1988).

Life in the Freezer: A Natural History of the Antarctic, by Alastair Fotherfill (Sterling, 1993).

The Peoples of the Arctic, by Kevin Osborn (Chelsea House, 1990).

Internet and Multimedia

Alaska Native Language Center and other departments of the University of Alaska at Fairbanks have several Web pages. Be sure to visit the on-line museum; (www.uaf.alaska.edu).

Antarctic Support Association supplies logistical support and training to stations in Antarctica. Site has news, background, images, and a catalog of polar clothing. ASA, 61 Inverness Dr. E, Suite 300, Englewood, CO 80112; 888–373-3946; (www.asa.org).

Arctic Circle has historical and cultural essays, a forum, and a museum. (www.lib.uconn.edu.80/ArcticCircle).

Bureau of Land Management has an informational Web site geared toward students; experiments included (www.blm.gov/education/arctic/northern).

Ice and Snow Data Base has searchable scientific data about ice and snow (www.muscat.co.uk/ccde/spri/icesnow).

The Journey North includes details about a 1994 arctic expedition by a team led by explorer Will Steger. Map, journal entries, statistics, and information on food, clothing, huskies, and other logistics (www.ics.soe.umich.edu/ed712/IAPIntro).

Penguin Pages is all about penguins (www.pobox.com/~penguins).

Polar Pointers is a vast listing of international Internet links about arctic and antarctic matters (www–bprc.mps.ohio–state.edu/polarpointers).

The South Pole Adventure Web Page, by prolific science writer and former teacher Janice VanCleave and Randy Landsberg, is geared toward students. It includes a travel log, the current weather report from the South Pole, experiments, questions and answers, and more. (www.southpole.com).

Sources of Curriculum and Hands-On Materials

Alaska Education provides information on polar science and culture, including curriculum materials (zorba.uafadm.alaska.edu/ankn/NPE).

Blue Ice: Focus on Antarctica is a seven-week on-line virtual field trip and teaching unit, including climate studies, geography, geology, biology, and more for grades 4-10. Registration required. Online Class, 935 McLean Ave, Suite 200, St. Paul, MN 55106; (www.onlineclass.com/BI/blueice).

National Geographic has sponsored many polar expeditions, including Robert E. Peary's quest for the North Pole in 1909, Richard Byrd's flyover of the South Pole in 1929, and explorer Will Steger's recent polar treks. National Geographic, P.O. Box 98199, Washington D.C. 20090; 800–548-9797; (www/nationalgeographic.com).

Teachers Experiencing Antarctica and the Arctic (TEA) is an educational program that sends teachers to polar regions to learn and participate in field studies. Site includes details on how to apply and other information: www.tea.rice.edu Also see Rice University's Glacier: Antarctic Earth Science site for background information: (www.glacier.rice.edu).

Who's at Home in the Animal Habitats? is an educational board game in which players must safely cross eight habitats, including a polar region, by answering two levels of questions about animal adaptation. Aristoplay, 450 S. Wagner Rd., Ann Arbor, MI 48103; 888-478-4263.

Sources of Photos and Maps

Antarctic Connection is an on-line store with maps, photos, posters, books, videos, links, and a daily weather report from the South Pole. The site also includes basic background on Antarctica (www.antarcticaconnection.com).

Arctic Perspectives sells a laminated wall map and other products. Arctic Perspectives, P.O. Box 75503, St. Paul, MN 55175 (www.arcticpersp.org).

Internet Geography Links: map generators, climate data, and more (ncgia.geog. buffalo.edu/GIAL/netgeog)

The Library of Polar and Ocean Maps has online political and relief maps of Antarctica and the Arctic Ocean (www.lib.utexas.edu/libs/PCL/map–collection/polar).

GLOSSARY

adapt: change to better suit the environment

Arctic Circle: the latitude above which there is at least one 24-hour day in summer

Counter-shading: a dark back and light belly, which camouflages many sea animals

Crustacean: hard-shelled sea invertebrate, such as krill

Glacier: a river of ice flowing from a highland to the sea

Iceberg: a chunk of ice that calves (breaks off) an ice sheet or glacier

Ice sheet: a huge blanket of ice that covers land or water for a long time

Insulate: keep heat in or out

Inuit (IN yoo it): Various bands of people who are native to the Arctic; formerly Eskimo

Migrate: move from one region to another to escape harsh weather or look for food

North Pole: 90° N; the top of the world

Permafrost: permanently frozen ground

South Pole: 90° S; the bottom the world

Taiga: arctic woodland

Tundra: treeless plain of the Arctic region

ANSWERS

Page 33: 1. Buffalo 2. Anchorage 3. Denver 4. Minneapolis 5. Boston
6. North Pole 7. Seattle 8. Charlotte 9. Atlanta 10. South Pole

Page 72: 1. Anchorage 2. Nome 3. Northwest
4. The area is mountainous and hard to cross.
5. The trail path must go around landforms such as rivers and mountains.

Page 34

Page 70

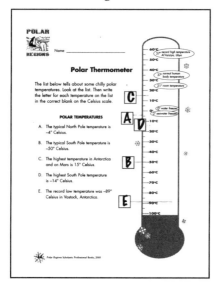

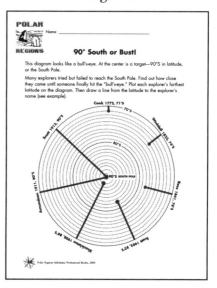